EARTH

NASA

EARTH

OUR CROWDED SPACESHIP

by ISAAC ASIMOV

Illustrated with photographs, maps and charts

THE JOHN DAY COMPANY/New York

An Intext Publisher

To all the world's children

Published with the cooperation of UNICEF and the United States Committee for UNICEF

The John Day Company, 257 Park Avenue South, New York, N.Y. 10010

Published on the same day in Canada by Longman Canada Limited.

Printed in the United States of America.

Library of Congress Cataloging in Publication Data

Asimov, Isaac, 1920-
  Earth: our crowded spaceship.

  SUMMARY: Discusses the problems faced by the Earth's inhabitants as population increases and energy sources, food, and land become more scarce.
  Bibliography: p.
  1. Human ecology—Juvenile literature. 2. Population—Juvenile literature. 3. Conservation of natural resources—Juvenile literature. [1. Human ecology. 2. Population. 3. Conservation of natural resources] I. Title.
GF48.A84   301.31   74-8967
ISBN 0-381-99625-3

CONTENTS

LIST OF ILLUSTRATIONS

PREFACE

Just for a moment, imagine that you are a first-class passenger on a huge spaceship traveling at a speed of 100,000 kilometers per hour. You discover that the ship's environmental system is faulty. Some passengers are dying due to poisonous gases in their oxygen supply. Also, there is a serious shortage of provisions—food supplies are being used up and the water supply is rapidly becoming polluted due to breakdowns in the waste and propulsion systems.

In the economy sections passengers are crowded together. Conditions are bad, especially for children. Many are seriously ill. The ship's medical officers are able to help few of the sick and medicines are in short supply.

Mutinies and fighting have been reported in some sections. Hopefully this conflict can be contained, but there is fear that the violence may spread into the other compartments.

The spacecraft has an overall destruct system, with the controls carefully guarded by a special technical crew. Unfortunately, the number of technologists who know how to set off the destruct system has increased, and there is great concern over what might happen if the fighting does spread.

We could go on, but the point is: What would you do if you were on that spaceship? Now that you have "imagined," are you ready to face reality? You are on such a spaceship right now—Spaceship Earth!*

*Donald Morris, "Developing Global Units for Elementary Schools," *International Education for Spaceship Earth* (New York: Foreign Policy Association, 1971).

The idea of our planet Earth as a spaceship may seem like science fiction, but what we have learned in this recent "space age" makes the idea more important as science fact. Do you know that everyone born since 1957—when the Russians launched the first satellite—is a member of the first generation of the space age? If you are seventeen years or younger, you are a part of that new generation, and this book is written especially for you.

Most people did not realize the importance of this new idea or concept about our planet at the beginning of the space age. In fact, it was about eleven years later—when the Apollo VIII astronauts sent back the first pictures of the Earth from the moon—that many people began to see and feel that all the Earth is really one small, self-contained system, with limited space and resources. On seeing these first pictures in December 1968, the poet Archibald MacLeish wrote that we "see ourselves as riders on the earth together . . . brothers who know now they are truly brothers."

But what about these riders or passengers on our planet? If space and resources, food, medicines, energy and raw materials are limited, how many riders can we crowd onto this planet? What kind of life and what kind of future will there be for the children living now and those soon to be born?

These are some of the questions Isaac Asimov makes you think about in this exciting book. They are also questions in which UNICEF, the United Nations Children's Fund, is very much interested. Since it was founded in 1946, eleven years before the space age began, UNICEF has worked hard to provide a future for the children of the world. Today UNICEF is helping millions of children in over a hundred developing countries. Boys and girls from a number of countries have shared, as some of you may have, in collecting for the Trick or Treat program or in other ways. But in many parts of the world the population is growing so fast that there are more sick, uneducated, malnourished children today than there were ten years ago.

Think of the size of the problem for a moment. In 1957 when the first satellite was launched, the world population was about 2.8 billion (2,800,000,000). By 1968 it had increased to about 3.5 billion (3,500,000,000). Today we have nearly 4 billion (4,000,000,000) passengers on our Spaceship Earth. To make the problem even greater, it is estimated that the number of children in the nations aided by UNICEF will increase by another 400 million before 1990! This would be like adding to the developing nations of the world twice the number of people we now have in the United States, and all of those would be children.

Unfortunately not everyone recognizes the problem. To some the idea of the Earth as a spaceship still seems unreal. They still feel and act as if the Earth has unlimited space and resources. In their view we live in a frontier society where we can just move on and spread out if things get too crowded. Some people have strong cultural, religious or economic beliefs about the importance of having large families. Others are afraid that there may be no children to care for them in old age or that there will be no sons to bear their family name. To some people just the very idea of family planning may be controversial.

Some may argue that there are areas of the world that are not crowded. This is true. In a few countries the growth rate is actually declining. But the overall problem of children in a crowded world is growing worse. UNICEF feels great concern over the implications of a rapidly increasing world population, because the children are the first to suffer when hunger, malnutrition and disease strike. In developing areas where population is growing most rapidly, nearly 1/3 of the children die of malnourishment before age four. Many millions more suffer extreme malnourishment, and over 10 million suffer such severe Vitamin A deficiency that they may become blind for life. Of those who survive, as many as nine out of ten have no access to health or medical care.

If the world is to solve such problems and provide a future for its children, many people will have to change some of their ideas about the size of their families and the distribution of the world's resources. This will not be easy. It is natural that people tend to resist change, or at least to change slowly. But our world has changed greatly during the past century. It is changing even more rapidly in this second half of the twentieth century—the space age.

When people's ideas, beliefs and customs lag behind the changes brought about by modernization and technology, we call this *culture lag*. However, we must also understand that some people feel the problem is not that their culture is lagging but that the world is changing too rapidly. The important thing to remember is that, either way you look at it, there is a conflict of ideas. Ideas are the powerful energy source that fuels the human mind and causes people to take action.

We believe in young people. We believe that you want to know more about population and resource problems aboard our Spaceship Earth. We believe that you will think carefully about these important ideas as you plan your own families and plan the wise use of resources. The future depends on you—the new space age generation!

Therefore, we are proud to join with the John Day Company in bringing you this book by Isaac Asimov, one of the world's leading writers of science fiction and science fact. The specific ideas and opinions expressed in the book are those of the author and do not necessarily reflect the views or policies of UNICEF, the U.S. Committee for UNICEF or any other national committee. However, we highly commend Mr. Asimov for his honest treatment of a most difficult and timely subject and for his contribution to population education for young people in this celebration of World Population Year and after.

C. Lloyd Bailey
Executive Director
U.S. Committee for UNICEF

1

PEOPLE

Look around you. What do you see?

You can see almost anything, depending on where you are. You might see a mountain with snow on top, or just snow, or a camel, or a palm tree, or a lot of automobiles, or the ocean or the inside of a building. One thing you are very likely to see, though, wherever you are, is other people.

If you are at home, you might see your mother and father, or your sisters and brothers, if you have any. If you are outside, you might see nobody at all, but it's more likely you'll see a few people, anyway. If you are in a city, you will probably see a great many people.

If you are at a bullfight, a baseball game or some great public celebration, you will see many thousands of people crowded so closely together you will see almost nothing else.

When you see a great many people in such a crowd, does it ever make you wonder how many people there may be in the whole world, altogether? Actually, nobody knows exactly, for it is difficult to count all those people. Some nations take a "census" every once in a while. When they do that, they count the number of people within their borders, and get other information as well.

The first nation to do this in modern times was the United States. It took its first census in 1790 and continued with another one every

ten years since then. Great Britain and France each started to take a census in 1801. Most of the nations in the world take censuses now, but they don't all do it very accurately and sometimes certain nations wait a long time between censuses. About twenty nations have never taken a census at all.

Still, suppose we start with the United States, which has a good record when it comes to taking censuses. According to the most recent American census, taken in 1970, the number of people in the United States as of April 1, 1970 was 200,255,151. That sounds very accurate, but actually it is quite possible that not everybody was counted. Even in the United States, which uses the most modern methods for counting people, some were probably missed (or maybe some people were counted twice).

Even so, we can make an "estimate" by taking a reasonable figure based on everything we know, without trying to make it too exact. We can say that the number of people in the United States (its "population") is about 210,000,000, as I write this book in 1974.

If we add in the censuses that other nations have taken, and make estimates for what has happened since those censuses were taken— and if we do our best to figure out reasonable populations for those nations that don't take censuses—we can get a figure for the total

world population. The best estimate that we can make is that in 1974 the world population is 3,800,000,000. That's three billion eight hundred million people.

The total number of people in the world is about nineteen times as many as the total number of people in the United States.

If you look at a map of the world (or better yet, at a globe) you will see that the United States spreads out over more of the world than most other nations do. It has a large "area"; so it's no wonder it has a lot of people in it.

Just the same, the United States is not the most populous nation in the world; that is, it does not have the most people. It is actually the fourth most populous nation. Three other nations, also large in area, are more populous.

The most populous nation in the world is China. It doesn't take censuses as often as the United States, so there is some argument as to just how many people there are in China. A reasonable estimate is that China now has a population of about 790,000,000. This is nearly four times as many people as the United States has. Just about 1/5 of all the people in the world live in China.

The second most populous nation is India, with 550,000,000 people, and then comes the Soviet Union with 250,000,000.

These four giant nations, China, India, the Soviet Union and the United States, have a total population of 1,790,000,000. This is nearly half of all the people in the world. The other half is divided up among about 150 nations, some of which are very small. There is one tiny nation called Nauru which occupies a small island in the Pacific Ocean. It has a total population of only 6,800.

Of course it isn't at all surprising that a huge nation like China should contain more people than a tiny nation like Nauru. It would make more sense if we figure out some way of talking about population that takes area into account also.

One way to do this is to imagine all the people in the world spread out evenly. Then we can calculate how many people there are in a

Children of many nations. *Photo: Unicef; photographer: Peter Larson*

The Earth is a small, self-contained system. *Photo: UNICEF*

particular bit of area. Instead of saying how many people there are altogether, we can talk about so many people in every bit of area of such and such a size. We call that the "population density."

For a particular bit of area suppose we use a "square kilometer"; that is, a square with each side one kilometer long. If you walk briskly, you can probably walk one kilometer in fifteen minutes.

That means you can walk all around the border of one square kilometer in an hour, or maybe even a little less than an hour. You see, then, that one square kilometer isn't a very big patch of land. In fact, the surface of the whole Earth has an area of about 510,000,000 square kilometers.

Of course, about 70 percent of the Earth's area is covered by ocean. People don't live on the ocean, except when they're on ships for a while, so we shouldn't count it as living area. That still leaves 150,000,000 square kilometers of land in the world.

Suppose we imagine that the 3,800,000,000 people of the world are spread out evenly over all the 150,000,000 square kilometers of land. In that case, there will be just about twenty-five people on every square kilometer of land. We can say then that the average population density on Earth right now is "twenty-five per square kilometer."

If we're going to do a lot of talking about population density, it might be convenient, and save writing time to use a shorthand way of saying "people per square kilometer." One way of doing that is to use the following abbreviation: $/km^2$. Then we can say that the average population density on Earth right now is $25/km^2$. That abbreviation still means that there are twenty-five people on every square kilometer of land surface, and you should still read it as "twenty-five people per square kilometer."

Let's look at the world's average population density another way. Suppose you are 160 centimeters tall and are standing on a large piece of very flat land. In every direction you see the horizon, the line where the land seems to meet the sky. From the height of your eyes, you see the horizon at a distance of about 4½ kilometers.

That means that as you turn around you can see a circle of land that is about sixty-five square kilometers in area. In all that space you could see, on the average, about 1,600 people. (Naturally, many of them would be inside houses.)

That is what you would see *on the average,* but you know that it's not what you would really see. There are places where you would

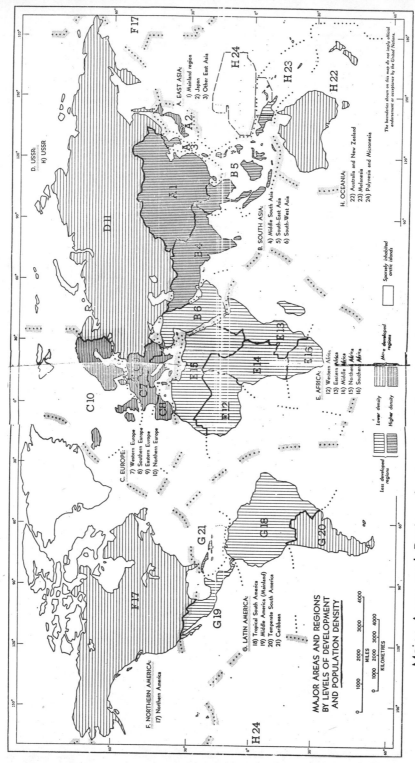

Major Areas and Regions by Levels of Development and Population Density. *Photo: United Nations*

MAJOR AREAS AND REGIONS
BY LEVELS OF DEVELOPMENT
AND POPULATION DENSITY

A. EAST ASIA:
1) Mainland region
2) Japan
3) Other East Asia

B. SOUTH ASIA:
4) Middle South Asia
5) South-East Asia
6) South-West Asia

C. EUROPE:
7) Western Europe
8) Southern Europe
9) Eastern Europe
10) Northern Europe

D. USSR:
11) USSR

E. AFRICA:
12) Western Africa
13) Eastern Africa
14) Middle Africa
15) Northern Africa
16) Southern Africa

F. NORTHERN AMERICA:
17) Northern America

G. LATIN AMERICA:
18) Tropical South America
19) Middle America (Mainland)
20) Temperate South America
20) Caribbean

H. OCEANIA:
22) Australia and New Zealand
23) Melanesia
24) Polynesia and Micronesia

Less developed regions
Lower density
Higher density

More developed regions
Lower density
Higher density

Sparsely inhabited arctic islands

The boundaries shown on this map do not imply official
endorsement or acceptance by the United Nations.

MILES
0   1000   2000   3000   4000

KILOMETRES
0   1000   2000   3000   4000

18

see far fewer than 1,600 people, and places where you would see far more than 1,600 people. The point is that the world's population is *not* spread out evenly.

Suppose you were standing somewhere on the large icy continent of Antarctica, which is in the neighborhood of the South Pole. You would not see anybody. Although Antarctica has an area of 14,000,000 square kilometers, it is so cold and unpleasant that no people live there at all. Occasionally, some scientists come to Antarctica for some weeks or months in order to study it, but that doesn't count. This means that Antarctica, which includes nearly 1/10 of all the land area in the world has an average density of population of $0/km^2$.

On the other hand, consider the little European nation of the Netherlands. It has an area of 32,600 square kilometers. It is only 1/450 as large as Antarctica, but it has a population of about 13,000,000. Its average density of population (if its people were spread out evenly over its area) would be $400/km^2$. This density is sixteen times the world average:

Now let's consider the population densities of the four giant nations of the world.

China has an area of 9,561,000 square kilometers. As far as area is concerned, it is the third largest nation in the world. China takes up 1/16 of all the land area of the world. If its 790,000,000 people were spread out evenly over its area, there would be eighty-two people in every square kilometer. China's average population density is $82/km^2$. This is over three times the world average, but it is only 1/5 the average population density of the Netherlands.

India has fewer people than China, but it has a considerably smaller area, too. India is only 3,268,000 square kilometers in area. There is so much less space in which to imagine its population spread over evenly that, although the Indian population is smaller than the Chinese, there are more Indians in each square kilometer of India than there are Chinese in each square kilometer of China. The average population density of India is 170/km^2. This is twice that of China, but is still less than half that of the Netherlands.

The Soviet Union is the largest nation in the world in area. It takes up 22,274,900 square kilometers, or about 1/7 of all the land area in the world. Its 250,000,000 people have so much room that the average population density of the Soviet Union is only 11/km^2. This is less than half the world average.

The United States is almost as large in area as China. The United States has an area of 9,363,000 square kilometers, but it has only a quarter of China's population. The average population density of the United States is about 21/km^2, which is just a little under the world average.

Just as some nations have a denser population than other nations, so within each nation there are regions that are more densely populated than other regions. Suppose we consider the United States, for instance, which is made up of fifty different states. The largest state, Alaska, has an area of 1,510,000 square kilometers. It includes 1/6 of all the land in the United States. However, it has the smallest population of any state in the United States—295,000.

The average population density in Alaska is only 0.2/km^2. (Does this sound as though there is only 1/5 of a person in every square kilometer? You don't have to imagine people divided into fifths. What 0.2/km^2 means is that there is, on the average, one person in Alaska for every five square kilometers of land.)

But what about Rhode Island, which is the smallest of the fifty states? Its area is only 3,140 square kilometers, but its population is 922,500, or three times the population of Alaska. The average population density in Rhode Island is 295/km^2, which is nearly 1,500 times as high as that of Alaska. Rhode Island is nearly twice as densely populated as India is, but is still only 3/4 as densely populated as the Netherlands.

People are most crowded in cities, of course. New York City has an area of 950 square kilometers. It is nearly 1/3 as large as the state of Rhode Island in area, but its population is 7,800,000, which is 8.5

Tokyo, one of the world's largest cities. *Photo: WHO; photographer: Takahara*

times as great as that of Rhode Island. The average population density of New York City is 8,200/km². The average population density of New York City is 400 times as great as that of the United States as a whole. It is even twenty times as densely populated as the Netherlands.

But even in New York City, there are differences in density. The city is made up of five boroughs, and the one with the smallest population is Richmond. Richmond has a population of 295,000 people and an area of 192 square kilometers. The average population density of Richmond is 1,530/km², only 1/5 of that of New York City as a whole.

Compare this with the borough of Manhattan, which has the smallest area of any of the five boroughs. The area of Manhattan is eighty-one square kilometers, but it has a population of 1,510,000. This means that the average population density of Manhattan is 18,600/km², which is more than twice that of New York City as a whole. Manhattan is forty-five times as densely populated as the Netherlands.

Every nation in the world has areas which are thinly populated and other areas which are more thickly populated. In the Soviet Union, the large Asian section known as Siberia has an average population density of only 4/km². The average population density of the Ukraine in the southwestern part of the Soviet Union is 80/km², which is twenty times as great as that of Siberia. In China, its westernmost province of Sinkiang has an average population density of only 5/km², while its coastal province of Kiangsu has one of 450/km², which is ninety times as great.

You can see, then, that though there are a great many people in the world, they are very unevenly distributed. There are vast areas such as Antarctica, Alaska and Siberia, where there are very few people. Most of the people in the world are crowded into a small part of the land area.

Does this mean that there is plenty of room for people to spread into? Perhaps not. The empty places are empty because they are very cold, or very dry, or very mountainous. People don't live in large numbers in Siberia or Alaska or Greenland or the Sahara Desert or Sinkiang or Antarctica, because it isn't very pleasant to live there. In fact, you might wonder if the various parts of the world aren't holding just about as many people as they can hold?

That's an interesting question. It is, perhaps, just about the most important question that is facing the world today. Does the world hold as many people as it can hold, or is there room for more?

In order to answer this question, it is not enough to know how many people there are in the world right now. It would help to know how many people there were in the world in past ages. We have to know whether the number of people in the world has always been about the same, or whether it has been changing. If it has been changing, we have to know how it has been changing.

Once we learn that, we might be able to estimate what the population will be like in the future. Then, perhaps, we can figure out where the world stands as far as population is concerned.

2

FIRE

In trying to find out what population was like in the past, we have no choice but to make guesses. Until 1790, when the United States began to take a census, nations hardly ever took any real censuses. Sometimes a ruler counted the fighting men of his nation. The Bible mentions several censuses of this kind in ancient Israel. Sometimes a ruler counted all the land and livestock that could be taxed. William I of England did this in 1086. Such counts are few and far between and cover only small areas. People who study population therefore have to make estimates based on whatever evidence they can find. They can never know for sure how nearly correct they are.

Suppose we go way back in time—say, about a million years ago, when human beings of the modern type did not yet exist. There were manlike beings called "hominids" living in Africa then. They had brains that were larger than those of apes but were not nearly as large as the brains of modern men. These early hominids lived very much as wild animals do today. They looked for food and they tried to avoid being killed and eaten by other animals. Perhaps there were only a few hundred thousand hominids alive at any one time.

The number of hominids didn't change much as time went on.

Suppose we imagine a tribe of them—let us say, fifty men, women and children. They would have some settlement and every

day they would wander about looking for food such as nuts, fruits or small animals that they could catch. If they could find food in plenty, they would be reasonably strong and healthy.

Some would die, of course, of old age or (much more likely) by accident, violence or disease. There would also be children born, of course. If there was a lot of food and if conditions were peaceful, there would be more children born than there would be people dying. The population would then go up. Instead of fifty hominids in the tribe, there would be sixty—seventy—eighty——

The more hominids in the tribe, the harder it would become to find enough food for all the members. The tribe would have to begin to hunt over a wider area. Perhaps they would have to move into the territory of another tribe and there would be fighting and they might be driven away. Some of the hominids would have to go hungry.

With less food for each person, some might die of starvation. Some might be so weakened that they wouldn't be able to fight off the various diseases that strike them. They might die in that way. There might be death by violence as one hominid fought another for scarce food.

With all that happening, it may be that people would begin to die faster than babies were born. The "death rate" would be higher than

A representation of pre-historic man. *Photo: Trustees of the British Museum (Natural History)*

the "birth rate," and that means the population would go down. It would go down to fifty again and perhaps further—forty—thirty——

As the number decreases, it becomes easier to find enough food for the fewer people that remain. The tribe could begin to grow stronger and be better off again, so the population goes up again. Sometimes there might be an unusually good group of years—good weather, lots of rain. The plants grow well and the animals become more numerous. In that case, the tribe may grow unusually numerous, too. There would be enough food for sixty or seventy people, year after year, instead of the usual fifty. Eventually, though, something is sure to happen to stop the rise. Bad weather comes or disease strikes or the food runs short.

At some other time, there may be a group of unusually bad years. The rains fail and there is a drought. Plants wither and the animals leave. Food is very scarce and perhaps most of the tribe starves. Eventually, though, the bad times end, too. The weather improves or what is left of the tribe manages to find some other location.

On the whole, then, the number of the hominids moves up and down, but their numbers average out. Sometimes, the numbers in one particular place might become unusually high for a while or unusually low, but for many thousands of years the world population of hominids may have stayed just about the same.

Why didn't it stay so forever? Why aren't there still only a few hundred thousand human beings?

The answer is that such an "equilibrium" in which the population neither rises nor falls depends on the outside world (or "environment") staying the same. Suppose the weather turns cold permanently and the glaciers come down from the north. Or suppose the weather turns very dry and the forest and grasslands where the hominids live turns into a desert and stays that way. Suppose a new kind of powerful and very deadly animal (or disease germ) invades the area. In that case, the number of hominids might drop all the

Drought-stricken West Africa. *Photo: UNICEF; photographer: Michael Palmer*

way down. There might even be none left, and the hominids would then be "extinct."

This happens now and then for the millions of species of plants and animals that have lived on the Earth through hundreds of millions of years. Many of them have suffered from a changing environment. Many species of plants and animals have become extinct because the places where they lived became too cold or too hot or too dry or too wet for them. Others became extinct because their food supply vanished or because new kinds of plants or animals arrived that fit the environment better.

Plants and animals change gradually, too, by a process called "evolution." They change in such a way as to be better suited to the environment, forming a slightly different kind of plant or animal. This new kind can do well and increase its numbers for a while. Thus, there was a time on Earth when giant reptiles died out and birds and mammals became the most successful life-forms.

Birds and mammals are better suited to most environments than the old reptiles had been because, for one thing, birds and mammals stay warm inside even in cold weather. Reptiles don't. This means that reptiles grow cold in winter, or at night, and can only move sluggishly then. Birds and mammals stay warm and remain active.

Mammals also have an advantage in having a larger brain than any other kind of animal has. This means they have a greater variety of ways in which to act in time of danger, and have a better chance of remaining alive. Hominids had very large brains even for mammals, so they did well. In fact, hominids were brainy enough to figure out ways of adjusting themselves to the environment without having to wait for evolutionary change, which is always very slow.

Suppose, for instance, hominids developed huge claws like a lion and used those claws to kill animals more easily than would be possible with ordinary fingernails. Claws could also be used to fight off dangerous large animals. If hominids had claws, they could get more food and be more secure. Once claws were developed, the hominid population would increase and stay increased. Of course,

The primitive wooden plow is still used today. *Photo: FAO; photographer: F. Botts*

it's not very likely that hominids would have developed huge claws through evolutionary change. If they did, it would take millions of years.

Suppose, though, that hominids were brainy enough to use stones as tools. They could tie a stone to a wooden handle by means of a tough vine and use such a weapon to kill small animals and to fight off large animals. Such a stone ax would do the work of claws and the idea for it could come in just a short time. There would be no need to wait millions of years for evolution to do something it might not do at all.

What's more, if hands developed claws, they wouldn't be useful for other purposes. If hominids used tools instead, those tools could always be changed for others. Different tools could be used for different purposes. All the tools could be put aside and the hand itself could be used.

Tools made it possible for hominids to do many things they couldn't do otherwise. Thanks to their large brains, hominids began to control the environment. Every new tool they devised helped make it easier to get food or ward off danger or both. That meant more hominids could stay alive and the population would go up. The control of the environment by the use of tools is called "technology." Each new tool is a "technological advance." Throughout history, technological advances have made it possible for population to increase.

The most remarkable technological advance that any hominid made in those very early times was the discovery of how to start and care for a fire. No other kind of living thing had ever learned how to do that. Hominids were using fire over 500,000 years ago and that was an enormous step toward controlling the environment.

For one thing, a fire gives off light and warmth. It made it possible for men to see at night, and it served to frighten off the large dangerous animals that prowled by night. Fire made it possible for hominids to endure the cold of night, or the cold of winter. Between that and the animal skins which hominids learned to wrap themselves in, hominids were able to move out of the tropical areas in which they had first evolved. That meant there were larger areas through which tribes of hominids might roam looking for food.

Then, too, hominids found that food, when heated by fire, became easier to chew and developed new flavors that seemed pleasant. This turned out to be very useful. Some foods which were too hard and coarse to make good eating became softer and easier to digest when they were heated. Cooking destroys bacteria and other parasites in food. This meant there would be less disease.

Through fire, then, hominids could get more food and be more secure. They could increase in numbers quite a bit above what would have been possible without fire. Thanks to fire, the population must have made a sudden jump to a new level in what is called a "population explosion." If all hominids everywhere in the world suddenly learned to use fire, the population might have gone up quickly. Knowledge of how to use fire must have spread very slowly, however, so that the population went up very slowly. The population explosion was a very small explosion.

About 300,000 years ago, a new kind of hominid evolved that we call "Homo sapiens." This is the kind of hominid that includes us. We are Homo sapiens. Every human being in the world today is Homo sapiens. There are no other kinds of hominids left alive.

Homo sapiens had a larger brain than any hominid that had ever lived, and he could develop new tools at a faster rate. Mankind spread over the face of the Earth faster than ever as a result. About

This woman is making a fire for cooking. *Photo: UNICEF*

25,000 years ago, Homo sapiens moved into the Americas and into Australia. Earlier species of hominids had never reached those continents. With more room to live in, the population continued to rise.

How high could the population rise? Even counting the possession of fire and tools, there was a limit. The population was bound to rise to the point where it became difficult to find enough food for everyone.

Through most of the history of mankind, people lived only on plants they happened to find, and on animals they found, caught and killed by hunting and fishing. This is a "food-gathering" way of life.

There are only so many plants and animals in a given area that people can eat. There is only so large an area that people can travel through in search of food each day. This means there is only a certain number of people that can exist on a given area at any one time. If more than that maximum somehow find their way into that area, they will eat up the plant and animal supply to the point where not enough would be left, after a while, and starvation would bring down the numbers.

This maximum number is not really very high. In 1492, when Columbus landed in the New World, the entire area that is now the United States was inhabited by people (who were named "Indians") living a food-hunting way of life. The usual estimate is that there were only 250,000 Indians living in the whole country. This is less than the number of people now living in New York City's Borough of Richmond. The average population density in the area in 1492 was only 0.025/km^2, or one person for every forty square kilometers.

If this is the sort of density of population that exists when people live by food hunting, the population of the whole world would be just about 4,000,000, or 1/2 the population of New York City today.

Of course, it's possible that the estimated number of Indians in the United States in 1492 is a little low. Or it's possible that the population density in Europe, Asia and Africa, where people had lived longer, might be higher than in the Americas. Some experts have tried to calculate how many people could possibly live in the world if food gathering was the only way of life. They don't all agree. Some think that 7,000,000 is the maximum, while some are willing to go as high as 20,000,000.

Well, let's do some supposing——

Let's suppose that about 310,000 years ago, there were only about 500,000 Homo sapiens in the whole world. Let's suppose that because they were spreading out and learning to use better tools, the population was rising—but very slowly. Let's suppose it rises so slowly that each year there is, on the average, a population increase of only 0.0007 percent. (That means that 0.0007 percent per year is the "growth rate" of the population.) This is a very small growth rate. It means that if there are 500,000 people to begin with, there are 500,001 two years later and 500,002 four years later.

Still, even with this tiny growth rate, if it continues year after year, the population will double after 100,000 years. If we begin with a population of 500,000 existing 310,000 years ago, it would become 1,000,000 at a period 210,000 years ago. This will double again and become 2,000,000 at a period 110,000 years ago. It will double still again and become 4,000,000 at a period 10,000 years ago, in 8000 B.C.

Suppose, then, that the world population in 8000 B.C. is 4,000,000 (so that the whole world is as densely populated at the United States area was in 1492). Suppose also that the growth rate continues to be 0.0007 percent per year. At that rate, it would take about 90,000 more years to reach a population of 7,000,000, which some people would think is the maximum that a food-gathering world can support. If we suppose that 20,000,000 was the maximum, it would take about 250,000 years to reach such a population.

But the growth rate did not continue at 0.0007 percent per year. It got considerably higher. The population shot up and, in just a few thousand years, went far beyond even the 20,000,000 mark.

What happened?

3

AGRICULTURE

About 8000 B.C. people, in what is now called the Middle East, made a new discovery. They found that it was not necessary to search for edible plants that happened to be growing here and there. It was possible to place the seeds of such plants in the ground and to take care of them while they were growing. Finally, they could be used for food when they were full-grown, ripened and then harvested. In this way, farming or "agriculture" was developed.

In the same way, it was not necessary to hunt for animals all the time. You could capture some animals, take care of them and encourage them to breed. In that way, you could have herds of animals. You could kill and eat some when you wanted to, and you could get milk, wool or eggs without killing them. In this way, "herding" was developed.

With plants and animals carefully preserved, a much larger food supply was available in a given area. Men removed other forms of life—weeds that would crowd out edible plants, animals that would eat the herds or their food. They turned as much of the environment as possible to the use of their cultivated plants and their domesticated animals.

People with more food in a particular area, ate better, lived longer and had more children. Population increased and so did

population density. In areas where there was farming and herding, the population density grew to be higher than the maximum possible in a food-gathering system. This was particularly true of farming because more food in the form of plants could be squeezed into a given area than in the form of animals.

The invention of agriculture came in the "Stone Age," the time when human beings were still using stone for their tools. It came toward the end of the Stone Age, though, when people had learned to make stone tools in a far more skillful fashion than in the ages that had come earlier. The earlier period was known as the "Old Stone Age." The later period is the "New Stone Age." Another name for the New Stone Age, using a Latin word, is "Neolithic Age."

When agriculture came into use in the Neolithic Age, it didn't come all by itself. Other things happened because of it. Agriculture meant, for instance, that the people who lived by growing plants had to stay in one place—where the plants were growing. They could no longer wander about looking for food.

What's more, people had to cooperate and work together to build irrigation ditches along the banks of rivers, in order to make sure that water would reach the plants even when the rains failed. Otherwise, everyone would starve. In this way, societies were built that

Indonesians stack their rice harvest. *Photo: UNICEF; photographer: Jack Ling*

were larger than the small family groups that existed when food gathering was the way of life.

Since food gatherers from outside the agricultural regions might try to raid the farms and take the food for themselves, the farmers had to huddle together for protection. They built their houses close together and put walls around them. Cities came into being for the first time, and this began what we call "civilization" (from a Latin word for "city").

With more and more people crowded together, there was more and more of a chance that someone would have a clever idea for a technological advance. With more and more people crowded together, any technological advance that was made would spread more rapidly. In fact, this is one of the rules of human history— technological advances encourage other technological advances so that technology has moved forward faster and faster and faster through all the centuries mankind has been on Earth. ——At least, so far.

Some of the technological advances in the early cities were in the form of war weapons, and this brings up another point. Technological advance has helped mankind to survive but it has also produced new dangers. Tools and weapons made it possible for man to stop being afraid of most animals. He had more reason to fear other men, however. The better the weapons of war became, the more bloody were the wars that were fought. Increasing numbers of deaths in warfare slowed the population rise that technology produced, but never stopped it altogether. ——At least, not so far.

But there was technological advance in directions other than war. The city dwellers learned how to put up elaborate buildings; they developed a system of writing and systems of religion; they learned to make pottery, to use wheels, to get metals out of rock.

The coming of agriculture, and all the technological advances that followed, made such a change in the human way of life that the period is sometimes described as the "Neolithic Revolution." The Neolithic Revolution meant a sudden rise in the rate at which population increased, since it provided both more food and greater security for those who were living in the places where the revolution took place.

Before agriculture, as I explained earlier, the growth rate might have been 0.0007 percent per year so that the population of the world would double only after 100,000 years. After agriculture, the growth rate increased to 0.035 percent per year, and it began to take only 2,000 years for the world population to double.

In other words, the Neolithic Revolution led to a second population explosion that was much larger than the first one that had followed the discovery of fire.

Naturally, the population explosion happened only in the areas where agriculture and the Neolithic Revolution took place. As the technology of the revolution spread, however, a larger and larger area of the world was able to support heavier populations. The total population of the world began to rise more and more rapidly, and most of that higher population was concentrated in the agricultural regions.

By 3000 B.C., agriculture had spread over three river valleys—the Tigris-Euphrates valley in Iraq, the Nile valley in Egypt and the Indus valley in Pakistan. These first civilizations were, at that time, just beginning to learn the use of metals, which was the next major technological advance.

The first metal that came to be used, in and about 3000 B.C., was copper. This was especially useful in the form of a mixture with tin, the mixture being called "bronze." Bronze was tougher and less brittle than stone, but it was also far less common. The people of the agricultural regions learned to get copper and tin from their rocky "ores" and used bronze for tools and weapons. They had entered the "Bronze Age."

By the time the agricultural regions of 3000 B.C. had entered the Bronze Age, the world population may have been something like 25,000,000, which meant an average world population density of some 0.16/km^2. This would be six times as much as it had been before the Neolithic Revolution, but it would still be only as many people as live in the nation of Ethiopia today.

This population rise was probably not confined to the agricultural regions only. When technological advances come in one section of the world, neighboring sections also benefit even though they don't make those advances themselves. The way of life in the neighboring sections changes somewhat and their population goes up, even if not by as much as in the regions that have actually developed the new technology.

Imagine people living between Egypt and Iraq in 3000 B.C. They might not be as technologically advanced as the agricultural people in the river valleys. They might not be as well-off or as comfortable. However, the people living between Egypt and Iraq would be able to trade with those regions and get tools and objects they couldn't make for themselves.

The amount of comfort a person can have in his life, the number of different things he can use, the advantage he can take of technology, can be called his "standard of living." The average standard of living in 3000 B.C. would be highest in the agricultural regions. It would be higher in a nonagricultural region near an agricultural region, however, than in a nonagricultural region far away from an agricultural region.

The agricultural regions in 3000 B.C., at the start of the Bronze Age, may have had an area of about 750,000 square kilometers. Add nearby regions which shared somewhat in the benefits, and we might have 1,000,000 square kilometers.

Half of the world population may have been found in that 1,000,000 square kilometers (only 1/150 of the total land area in the world) in 3000 B.C. The population density there would be 12/km^2. In the rest of the world it would be 0.08/km^2. Population density in the agricultural regions would be 150 times that in the nonagricultural areas. This, of course, is just a very rough estimate.

As time went on, the knowledge of agriculture spread out over most of Europe, Asia and northern Africa. The art of producing and using bronze spread out behind it.

Somewhere about 1200 B.C. people in eastern Asia Minor learned how to produce iron from rocky ores containing it. Iron is more difficult to get than copper and tin are. The ores have to be heated to higher temperatures. Still iron is more common, once you learn how to get it, and it is harder and tougher than bronze is.

Starting in 1200 B.C., the agricultural areas shifted from bronze tools and weapons to iron tools and weapons. The world was at the beginning of the "Iron Age." By that time, the world population was about 70,000,000, and the average population density for the world was now about $0.5/km^2$. This was three times what it was at the beginning of the Bronze Age and seventeen times what it was at the beginning of the Neolithic Revolution.

Not only was population continuing to increase as technology advanced, but it was increasing faster and faster as knowledge of agriculture and other advances spread to wider and wider areas of the world. By the time the Iron Age began, the growth rate of population had become about 0.05 percent per year. It would now take only 1,400 years for the world population to double.

By 100 A.D., the ancient world reached a peak of development. Nations had grown larger and larger as some conquered others. "Empires" were established, with one nation ruling over many others. The largest and most successful empire of ancient times, at least in the Western world, was the Roman Empire. It included large sections of southern Europe, western Asia and northern Africa.

In 100 A.D., the Roman Empire was at its largest size and had an area of about 4,000,000 square kilometers, with a population of about 50,000,000—twice as much as the population of the entire world at the opening of the Bronze Age. The average density of population over the entire Roman Empire was $12/km^2$.

The average life expectancy in the Roman Empire may have reached twenty-two years. In the more prosperous provinces it may even have been thirty to thirty-five years for limited periods of time. This is as high as it ever got before modern times.

Trisno works with his father in their small rice paddy.
Photo: UNICEF; photographer: Jack Ling

Agriculture had spread to eastern Asia in quite ancient times and by 100 A.D. there was a Chinese Empire that was as large as the Roman Empire and had as large a population. There, too, the average population density was about 12/km^2.

The rest of the world outside the Roman and Chinese Empires by now had another 50,000,000 population. It was that high because the regions between the Chinese and Roman Empires were also agricultural and also had undergone considerable technological advance. Those regions included Persia and India, for instance. There were also agricultural regions in Europe north of the Roman Empire, and in the Americas as well (in central Mexico and in Peru).

The developed regions outside the two great Empires may have had a total area similar to that of the Roman Empire and a total population almost like it. We might, therefore, say that in 100 A.D., 12,000,000 square kilometers of the world's land surface were occupied by people who depended on agriculture for their livelihood. The agricultural regions made up about 1/13 of the total land surface and contained a population of 150,000,000 people, twice as many as the whole world contained at the beginning of the Iron Age.

The world outside the agricultural areas may have had a population of 10,000,000 or so. The total world population was about 160,000,000 then and the average population density for the whole world had finally reached the figure of $1/km^2$.

The average population density of the agricultural areas in 100 A.D. was probably similar to the average population density of the agricultural areas in 3000 B.C. — $12/km^2$. The actual technology of agriculture had not improved very much in those 3,000 years, and the population growth was due entirely to the spreading outward of agriculture. It wasn't that there was *better* farmland producing more food; it was just that there was *more* farmland producing more food.

To be sure, the figure of $12/km^2$ is only an average. In any large region supported by agriculture, there will always be the fertile areas which will be pockets of higher population density, but these will be balanced by rocky or sandy or dry areas where there will be lower population density.

Thus, in the Roman Empire, the population density along the Nile River or in Syria or in parts of Italy was considerably higher than $12/km^2$, but the population density in outlying provinces like Spain and Britain was considerably lower than $12/km^2$.

Suppose we stick to an *average* population density of $12/km^2$ and ask how many people in the world an agricultural way of life can support. Since regions acquainted with agriculture in 100 A.D. made up only 1/13 of the whole land surface, we might suppose that once the whole world began to depend on agriculture, the total population might be thirteen times what it was in 100 A.D.

This means that a completely developed agricultural world might support nearly 2,000,000,000 people. This is a hundred times as great as the 20,000,000 people that a food-gathering world could support at the most generous estimate. And, to be sure, population continued to grow after 100 A.D. even though both the Roman Empire and the Chinese Empire began to lose strength.

After 400 A.D., western Europe was overrun by German war bands, and there was a decline in many aspects of civilization. For about 500 years, there was what was called a "Dark Age" in western Europe. Population declined in those centuries in western Europe and the standard of living fell. Many history books treat the Dark Age as though it were worldwide, because so many history books have been written by West Europeans and their descendants. Actually, during all that period, southeastern Europe and most of Asia continued to be prosperous. The population of the world in general continued to rise even though that of western Europe declined.

The western European Dark Age did not decline in technology as much as one might think. Even when empires fall apart—and art, literature and theoretical knowledge seem to be in the doldrums— technological knowledge tends to hang on. Technology is too important to everyday life for it to be forgotten. By 1000 A.D., tech-nology was actually moving ahead in western Europe. It quickly went beyond what had existed in the Roman Empire, and population began to rise quickly even in those lands that had just gone through a Dark Age.

The biggest blow to human population ever recorded in history took place in the 1300s. In that century, the deadliest disease epidemic ever known struck mankind. It was the "Black Death." It started somewhere in central Asia and spread rapidly. In 1347 it reached western Europe, and over a period of three years it may have killed as many as 25,000,000 people. It probably killed considerably more than that in Asia and Africa.

Suppose it killed 75,000,000 people altogether. This is quite possible, and it may well have killed more than that. But even if it were only 75,000,000 people who were killed, that would include 1/6 of all the people then on Earth and they would have died in the space of ten years. At no other time in history, as far as we know, did so large a fraction of the human population die in so short a time.

Yet mankind survived even that blow. It took a century to recover, but by 1450 the population was back to where it had been before the Black Death, and it then continued moving upward.

In the 1400s, the mariner's compass was in wide use in European ships. This meant that European ships could make long voyages out of sight of land without getting lost. Europeans began to explore the world in a way that nobody had ever done before. By 1500, European vessels had reached the Far East and had discovered the American continents.

Also in the 1400s, Europeans had worked out the technology of printing. This meant the publishing of more books and the faster spread of knowledge of all kinds. It meant that new advances in technology could be made more easily and spread more quickly. With that, the people of western Europe became the most technologically advanced people in the world. They and their descendants have stayed in the lead ever since.

This was especially true in the field of warfare, for in the 1400s, Europeans had developed the use of gunpowder in cannon. Soon they made themselves militarily stronger than any other people in the world.

By 1600, then—despite the fall of the Roman Empire, and various other periods of warlike trouble, and also despite the terrible blow of the Black Death—the world population stood at about 500,000,000 people. This was over three times what it had been in 100 A.D., and the average population density for the world was now about 3.3/km^2.

Despite plagues and troubles, population had not only been going up, but it had been going up faster than ever before. After 100 A.D., the world population growth rate was, on the average, at 0.08

percent per year. This meant the world population was increasing at a rate that would double it in only 900 years.

In 1600, the people, in about a quarter of the world's land area, were being supported by agriculture, and the fraction was still going up. Through the 1500s and afterward, Europeans were pouring into the American continents. There the Indian civilizations in Mexico and Peru had been destroyed, and the food-gathering Indians in the rest of the continents were being pushed back or killed by large numbers of agricultural invaders from Europe. Later on, Australia, New Zealand, southern Africa and other regions were settled by Europeans.

The result was that the world population was about 550,000,000 in 1650; about 730,000,000 in 1750; and about 900,000,000 in 1800.

In 1800 the world population was nearly twice what it had been in 1600. Thanks to the new lands available to European farmers, the world population after 1600 had been increasing at a growth rate of nearly 0.3 percent per year. Such an enormous growth rate had never been experienced before and it meant that the world population was increasing in a way that would cause it to double in only 250 years.

If the world population continued to increase at a rate of nearly 0.3 percent a year, it would mean that, by 2050 A.D., a world population of 2,000,000,000 would have been reached. That would probably have been the limit that an agricultural world could support.

That is not the way things turned out. The growth rate for world population did *not* stay at nearly 0.3 percent per year. It got larger, much larger. The world population went far beyond the 2,000,000,000 mark long before 2050.

What's more, this took place without people everywhere being reduced to starvation due to shortage of food. Indeed, the standard of living actually went up over most of the world.

What happened?

4

INDUSTRY

In the late 1700s something happened in Great Britain. The British were running out of wood on their narrow island, and they needed wood badly. They needed wood to build houses and ships and many other things. The trouble was they also needed to burn wood in order to heat their houses and to make iron out of iron ore.

As far as burning was concerned, there was a substitute. They turned to coal. But coal had to be dug out of the ground and in Great Britain's damp, rainy climate, the mines sometimes filled with water. The water had to be pumped out. It was very difficult to do that by using the muscles of human beings and animals.

Fortunately, a practical "steam engine" was developed in 1769. Some of the coal was burned, and the heat of the burning coal turned water into steam. The steam was trapped, and as it expanded it could be made to turn a wheel that ran a pump. It was soon found that steam engines could be made to run many other things besides pumps. They could run machinery in factories, for instance, and by 1800, there began what is called the "Industrial Revolution."

In this Industrial Revolution, machinery could be made to do the work men had been doing. A few human beings, using machines powered by steam engines, could do more work on farms and in factories than many men without machines could have done. This

meant more food and other goods, while more human beings—not needed in the farms and factories—were free to do other things. There were more people studying science, for instance, and thinking up inventions. Technology began to advance more rapidly than ever, and there began the third and largest population explosion.

In the early 1800s, inventors showed how the steam engine could move ships across water against wind and current. They showed how coaches could be moved over rails without the use of horses. Steamships and steam locomotives were able to move human beings over the face of the land and water faster than ever before. The steam engine could turn a wheel through a magnetic field, and a current of electricity could be formed. As the 1800s went on, more and more uses were found for electricity.

As nations grew industrialized they could sell their goods abroad in return for food and ore and other raw materials. The goods produced by industrial nations were needed so badly by the rest of the world that they could be sold at a great profit. The industrialized nations grew rich. They didn't have to grow much food; they could buy it from other nations and have more food than they ever had before.

Industrialized nations could move food rapidly by steamship and

steam locomotive. If there were food shortages in one place, more food could be brought in. Famines became very uncommon.

Of course, famines continued in nations that were nonindustrialized. About 2,500,000 people died in Ireland in 1846, and many more died of starvation in India and China in the 1800s. Even today, it is estimated that 15,000 people die of starvation each day. What's more, 2/3 of the world's population have hardly enough to eat and are hungry most of the time.

Then, too, through advances in science, it was discovered in the 1860s that diseases were often caused by germs. Doctors learned how to fight germs and there were fewer deaths by disease. Of course, disease wasn't entirely wiped out. In 1918, 100,000,000 people died in a worldwide influenza epidemic. This was more people, perhaps, than died in the Black Death, yet it was not as serious as far as population was concerned. The influenza epidemic of 1918 killed less than 5 percent of the people living on Earth at that time, but the Black Death killed more than 15 percent.

(*Left*) Women work with mechanical spinning machines, in India. *Photo: United Nations*

(*Right*) This child, in India, suffers from malnutrition. *Photo: UNICEF*

In other words, although famine and disease continued to kill after the Industrial Revolution, they were killing smaller percentages of the world's population. With smaller percentages of people dying of starvation and disease, it meant that the average life expectancy of people in the world was rising.

Until 1850, the average life expectancy was not more than thirty-five years anywhere in the world. In the most prosperous places, one-year-old infants who had survived the dangerous first year of life had only an even chance of living beyond thirty-five years. By the time thirty-five years had passed, half would be dead.

The life expectancy in Europe in 1850 was possibly no higher than it had been in parts of the Roman Empire, eighteen hundred years before, or even in parts of Egypt four thousand years before. There were particular individuals who lived to be seventy, eighty or even ninety years of age in Europe in 1850, or in ancient Rome or in ancient Egypt. Such great ages were very rare, however.

Once germ diseases began to be conquered, the life expectancy began to rise in those regions where the Industrial Revolution was taking place. By 1900, the life expectancy in the United States was forty-seven. Half the people who survived the first year of life could expect to live nearly half a century. The world had never seen such a thing, but it didn't stop there. In the United States, today, the life expectancy is sixty-nine years for men and seventy-three years for women. In Norway, today, it is seventy-one years for men and seventy-five years for women.

To be sure, people who reach seventy nowadays are just as old as people who reached seventy in previous centuries, and they have no greater chance of living to be one hundred. However, many more people live to be seventy nowadays than in any previous century. We can put it this way. In passing from food hunting to agriculture, the life expectancy had doubled. In passing from agriculture to industrialization, the life expectancy had doubled again. Another way of saying that life expectancy increases is to say that the death rate decreases.

Before industrialization, it was common for the death rate to be 35 per thousand per year. This means that out of every thousand men, 35 die in the space of one year. After industrialization, and particularly after the coming of modern medicine, the death rate began to drop rapidly.

In the United States where the death rate may have been 35 per thousand in 1800, it was down to 15.5 per thousand in 1900, and is down to 9.5 per thousand now. There are places in the world where the death rate is as low as 7 per thousand. Industrialization, and the advances in technology and medicine that followed, meant, in other words, a faster and faster increase in population as fewer people died and more people lived to have more babies.

In 1850, just before the germ theory of disease was worked out, the world population was about 1,200,000,000, but by 1900 it was 1,600,000,000. In 1900 the world population was nearly twice as high as it had been in 1800, and it was moving up faster than ever. In the 1800s, population growth rate was 0.7 percent per year, which was twice as high as it had been in the 1700s. Population in the 1800s was increasing so fast that the number of people in the world could be expected to double in about one hundred years.

Then, after 1900, the growth rate continued to rise and began to push a figure of 0.9 percent per year. The growth rate in the beginning of the 1900s was such that the world population could be expected to double in only seventy-five years. And the growth rate still continued to go higher.

In 1920 the world population was 1,800,000,000, and in 1930 it was 2,000,000,000. The world population in 1930 was the maximum the world could have supported if the Industrial Revolution had never happened. Those 2,000,000,000 would have been starving without industrialization. Instead, they had an average standard of living higher than the world had ever seen and population was still going up faster than ever. In 1940 the world population was 2,250,000,000, and in 1950 it was 2,510,000,000.

The 1900s saw disasters of various kinds, but nothing seemed to be bad enough to stop the population rise. In fact, nothing after the Black Death had succeeded in doing that.

There were 8,000,000 dead in World War I from 1914 to 1918; 20,000,000 dead in World War II from 1939 to 1945; 100,000,000 dead in the influenza epidemic of 1918. It made little difference. The population might decrease in the immediate areas where these disasters were worst, but once the crisis was past, population started going up again. And population had been going up all the time in other places. The population growth rate had risen so high in the 1900s that almost any disaster could be made up for very quickly. Even the influenza epidemic of 1918, horrible though it was, made hardly any dent in the population rise.

Industrialization was spreading. In the 1900s, for instance, Russia and Japan were industrialized. The same thing happened to them that had happened to the nations that had been industrialized earlier. The death rate in the Russian Empire in 1900 was thirty per thousand, for instance, but today in the Soviet Union (as the nation is now known) the death rate has dropped to ten per thousand.

After 1950, even nonindustrial regions began to benefit from the advances of science and medicine in the industrial nations. The death rate in a nonindustrial nation such as Mexico is now only twelve per thousand, for instance.

So the growth rate of world population which had been nearly 1 percent per year in the early 1900s climbed higher still to 1.2—1.4—1.6 percent per year. The time it would have taken the world population to double dropped to sixty—fifty—forty years.

By 1960, the world population was 3,000,000,000; by 1970, it was 3,600,000,000; and now it is 3,800,000,000. At the present moment (1974) the world population is nearly twice what it was in 1930 and is over four times what it was in 1800 when the Industrial Revolution was in its beginnings. What's more, the growth rate of world population is now a full 2 percent per year. If this continues, the world population will double in only thirty-five years.

At the beginning of this book, all I could say was that the population of the world is 3,800,000,000. Now we see more clearly where we are. Not only is the population of the world far greater than it has ever been, but it is increasing to still higher levels at a far faster rate than it has ever been increasing in the entire history of the world.

We can look at this in another way. Let us start at the beginning of the Agricultural Age, where there were only half as many people in all the world as there are in New York City today. It took 10,000 years for the world population to reach the 1,000,000,000 mark. That was reached about 1810.

It then took only 120 years for the world to add another billion people and reach a population of 2,000,000,000. That mark was reached in 1930. It then took only 30 years to reach the 3,000,000,000 mark in 1960. Only 15 years will be needed to reach the 4,000,000,000 mark in 1975.

Is this the way it will keep going? Will the world keep adding billion after billion, faster and faster? How long can we keep it up?

5

LIMITS

Earlier in the book I said that a food-gathering world could only support 20,000,000 people at most, and that an agricultural world could only support 2,000,000,000 people at most.

What about an industrial world? Is there now a new limit? Suppose the whole world became industrialized and that industry and science worked very carefully and very well. How many people could such a world support?

Different numbers have been suggested, but the highest figure I have seen is 20,000,000,000. This is ten times the population an agricultural world could support, and a thousand times the population a food-gathering world could support.

Let us suppose 20,000,000,000 is the limit, then. How long would it be before the world contained 20,000,000,000 people?

That depends on how the world's population growth rate rises or falls. The growth rate might slow down or even reverse if there are terrible wars, famines or epidemics. (Naturally, everyone hopes such disasters won't happen.) On the other hand, the growth rate might rise even further. So far in history, the growth rate has been going up steadily from 0.0007 percent or less before the coming of agriculture to 2.0 percent now. Yet a 2 percent growth rate is not the highest possible. There are nations in the world with a growth rate of

3.5 percent, and with population increasing at this rate it will double in only twenty years.

We can't be sure, then, whether the growth rate will go up or down in the future. Just for the sake of argument, and to keep things simple, let's suppose the growth rate will stay exactly what it is now. If it does, how long will it take the world to increase its population to 20,000,000,000?

If the present world population of 3,800,000,000 doubles, that will make it 7,600,000,000; and if it doubles again, the population will be 15,200,000,000. Since each doubling, at a growth rate of 2.0 percent, takes thirty-fives years, it will take seventy years altogether to reach the 15,200,000,000 mark. Then, fifteen more years will bring the world population to 20,000,000,000. At the present growth rate, in other words, our planet will contain all the people that an industrialized world may be able to support by about 2060 A.D.

Some young people who are alive today may someday have children who will live to see the world of 2060. It may be a world of 20,000,000,000 people, over five times as many as there are today. If this is all an industrial world can support, those people will be living at a starvation level—just barely keeping alive. Surely, that is not a pleasant outlook for a time only eighty-five years from now.

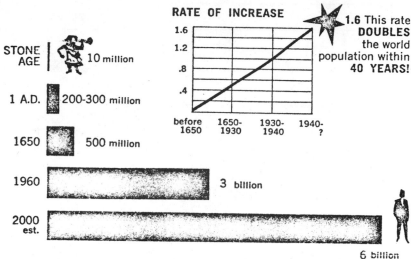

RATE OF INCREASE

1.6 This rate **DOUBLES** the world population within **40 YEARS!**

STONE AGE		10 million
1 A.D.		200-300 million
1650		500 million
1960		3 billion
2000 est.		6 billion

How the World's Population Has Grown.

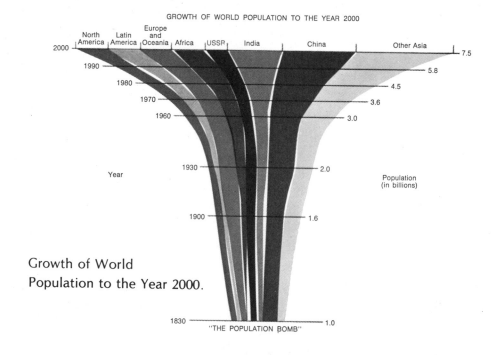

GROWTH OF WORLD POPULATION TO THE YEAR 2000

North America | Latin America | Europe and Oceania | Africa | USSR | India | China | Other Asia

2000 — 7.5
1990 — 5.8
1980 — 4.5
1970 — 3.6
1960 — 3.0
1930 — 2.0
1900 — 1.6
1830 — 1.0

Year

Population (in billions)

"THE POPULATION BOMB"

Growth of World Population to the Year 2000.

But wait, perhaps we aren't allowing for changes in the way human beings live.

Let's go back to the food-gathering world. At that time, 20,000,000 would have been the population limit of the world, yet long before that figure was reached, the world stopped being just food gathering. Agriculture was developed, and the population zoomed right past the 20,000,000 mark. Instead of people starving, the average standard of living rose.

The population limit in an agricultural world would have been 2,000,000,000, but long before that figure was reached, the world stopped being just agricultural. The Industrial Revolution took place, and the population zoomed right past the 2,000,000,000 mark. Instead of people starving, again the standard of living rose.

Well, then, is there any reason to be worried now? Before the new 20,000,000,000 mark is reached, might we not expect something else to happen that will make it possible for the population to zoom right past it with the standard of living still rising?

Let's see——

At the time that agriculture was first introduced, the world contained about 1/5 of the people it could hold at most. If agriculture had not been invented, it might have taken perhaps 250,000 years for the food-gathering world to reach its limit.

At the time the Industrial Revolution began, the world contained about 1/2 the people it could hold at most. If the industrialization of the world had not begun, it would have taken about 250 years for the agricultural world to reach its limit.

Now the world has, perhaps, less than a fifth of the people it could hold, if it is really true that 20,000,000,000 is the industrial limit. Yet the growth rate has grown so high that there is only eighty-five years left for that limit to be reached. In short, every time there is a great change that makes it possible for the world to hold more people, there is less time for that change to happen. And there are far more people to suffer if anything goes wrong.

What's more, each new change comes after a shorter and shorter time. Mankind remained in the food-gathering stage for hundreds of thousands of years before agriculture was introduced. Then mankind stayed in the agricultural age for 10,000 years before industrialization began. But the Industrial Age will have lasted only about 300 years before another great change seems to have become necessary. The next age will then perhaps only last fifty years before still another must come about.

Suppose we decide to hope for the best, however. Let us suppose that a change *will* take place in the next seventy years and that there will be a new age in which population can continue rising to a far higher level than we think it can now. This means that there will be a new and higher limit, but before that is reached, still another change will take place, and so on. Let's suppose that this sort of thing can just keep on going forever.

Is there any way of setting a limit past which nothing can raise the human population no matter how many changes take place?

Suppose we try to invent a real limit; something so huge that no one can imagine a population rising past it. Suppose we imagine that there are so many men and women and children in the world that altogether they weigh as much as the whole planet does. Surely you can't expect there can be more people than that.

Let us suppose that the average human being weighs sixty kilograms. If that's the case then 100,000,000,000,000,000,000,000 people would weigh as much as the whole Earth does. That number of people is 30,000,000,000,000 times as many people as there are living now.

It may seem to you that the population can go up a long, long time before it reaches the point where there are 30,000,000,000,000 times as many people in the world as there are today. Let's think about that, though. Let us suppose that the population growth rate stays at 2.0 percent so that the number of people in the world continues to double every thirty-five years. How long, then, will it take for the world's population to weigh as much as the entire planet?

The answer is—not quite 1,600 years. This means that, by 3550

A.D., the human population would weigh as much as the entire Earth. Nor is 1,600 years a long time. It is considerably less time than has passed since the days of Julius Caesar.

Do you suppose that perhaps in the course of the next 1,600 years, it will be possible to colonize the Moon, and Mars and the other planets of the solar system? Do you think that we might get many millions of people onto the other worlds in the next 1,600 years and lower the population of the Earth itself?

Even if that were possible, it wouldn't give us much time. If the growth rate stays at 2.0 percent, then in a little over 2,200 years, say, by 4220 A.D., the human population would weigh as much as the entire solar system, including the sun.

We couldn't escape to the stars, either. Even if we could reach them, even if we could reach *all* of them, population would reach a limit. If the growth rate stays at 2.0 percent, then in 4,700 years, by about 6700 A.D., the human population would weigh as much as the entire known universe.

So you see we can't go on forever at the rate we are going. The population rise is going to have to stop somewhere. We just can't keep that 2.0 percent growth rate for thousands of years. We just can't, no matter what we do.

Let's try again, and let's be more reasonable. Suppose we go back to considering the density of population on Earth.

Right now, the average density of population on Earth is 25/km². If the population of the world doubles then the average density of population also doubles, since the area of the world's surface stays the same. This means at a population growth rate of 2.0 percent per year, the average density of population in the world will double every thirty-five years.

In that case, if the growth rate stays where it is, how long will it take for the average density of population to become 18,600/km²? Such a density is almost 750 times as high as the present density, but it will be reached, at the present growth rate, in just about 340 years. Of course, this density is reached only if human beings are confined to the land surface of the world. Perhaps human beings will learn to live on the bottom of the ocean or on great platforms floating on the sea. There is more than twice as much ocean surface as there is land surface, and that would give more room for people.

That wouldn't do much good, however. At the present growth rate, it would take only forty-five additional years to fill the ocean surface, too. In 385 years, the average density of population would be $18,600/km^2$ over land and sea both. That would be by about 2320 A.D. But a density of $18,600/km^2$ is the average density of population of the island of Manhattan.

Imagine a world in which the average density everywhere—over land and sea alike, *everywhere,* in Antarctica and Greenland, over the oceans and along the mountains, over the entire face of the globe—was equal to that of Manhattan. There would have to be skyscrapers everywhere. There would be hardly any open space. There would be no room for wilderness, or for any plants and animals except those needed by human beings. Very few people would imagine a world like that could be comfortable, yet at the present growth rate we will reach such a world in only 385 years.

But let's not pick Manhattan. Let's try the Netherlands. It is a pleasant, comfortable nation, with open land and gardens and farms. It has a standard of living that is very high and yet its average population density is $400/km^2$. How long would it take for our population to increase to the point where the average density of the surface of the world, sea and land, would be $400/km^2$?

The answer is 200 years, by about 2175 A.D.

You see, then, that if you don't want to go past the average population density of the Netherlands, we can't keep our present growth rate going even for hundreds of years, let alone thousands. In fact, we might still be arguing in an unreasonable way. Can we really expect to have a worldwide Netherlands in the next 200 years?

No one really believes that mankind can spread out over the ocean bottom or the ocean top in the next 200 years. It is much more likely that he will stay on land. To be sure, there may be some

This Nigerian boy's most precious possession is his camel. *Photo: UNICEF; photographer: Alain Massin*

people who would be living offshore in special structures, on the sea or under it. They would make up only a small fraction of all mankind. Almost everybody will be living on land.

Then, too, not every place on land is desirable. It isn't at all likely that there will be very many people living in Antarctica or in Greenland or in the Sahara Desert or along the Himalaya Mountain range over the next 200 years. There may be some people living there, more people than are living there now, but they will represent only a small fraction of the total population.

In fact, most of the Earth's land surface isn't very suitable for large populations. At the present moment, most of the Earth's population is squeezed into that small portion of Earth's land surface that is not too mountainous, too dry, too hot, too cold or too generally uncomfortable. In fact, 2/3 of the world's population is to be found on a little over 1/13 of the land surface of the planet. About 2,500,000,000 people are living on 11,000,000 square kilometers of land that can best support a high population. The average density on the 11,000,000 square kilometers of the best land is $230/km^2$, while the average density of the rest of the land surface is just under $10/km^2$.

Suppose the population continues to increase at the present growth rate and the distribution remains the same. In that case, after thirty years, the average population density of the less pleasant parts of the Earth will reach the $19/km^2$ figure, but the density of the 11,000,000 square kilometers of best land will be $400/km^2$.

In other words, we will reach a kind of worldwide Netherlands density figure, for as far as we can go, in only about thirty years.

But will all the world be as well-organized and as prosperous as the Netherlands is now? Some of the reasons that the Netherlands is as well off as it is now, is that it has a stable government, a highly educated population, and a well-organized industrial system.

This is not true of all nations, and they need not expect to be as well off as the Netherlands when they are as crowded as the Netherlands. Indeed, if they have an agricultural way of life and a poorly educated people, who don't have long traditions of stable government, then a population as dense as that of the Netherlands now is, would only bring misery. In other words, the world can't keep going at the present growth rate, even for tens of years, let alone for hundreds or thousands.

The matter of a population limit is not a problem for the future, then. We might as well realize that the world is just about reaching its population limit *now*.

Of course, the entire argument in this chapter is based on the supposition that the population growth rate will stay the same as it is now. Suppose the growth rate drops. Won't that give us more time before the limit is reached? In fact, if it drops to zero, the population will stop growing and the limit will never be reached.

It would be useful, then, to look at the growth rate in more detail and see what the chances are of its dropping.

6

GROWTH RATE

If we think of population *now,* what do we see?

The world population is 3,800,000,000. At a 2.0 percent growth rate, this means that in the next year the world population will increase by 76,000,000, an amount equal to the population of West Germany and East Germany put together.

Another way of putting it is that the world's population is increasing at 200,000 each day, or 140 each minute. Every second that passes means two additional people added to the world's population. And, of course, this figure goes up every year as there are more and more people in the world. In 1990 there will be three additional people added to the world's population every second, and in 2010, four additional people.

But where are all these additional people being added? Surely they are not being added equally everywhere on Earth. There are few people in the Sahara Desert and few babies are being born there. There are many people in China, and many babies are being born there. (Of course, a high growth rate doesn't just mean that many babies are being born. If many people die, the population doesn't grow. What counts is how many *more* people are born than people who die.)

If the growth rate were the same all over the world, matters would

be simple. The more people in a particular nation, the more additional people would be added to the population in a particular amount of time.

If the growth rate were 2.0 percent per year everywhere, then a nation of 1,000,000 people would grow by 20,000 in one year; a nation of 100,000,000 people would grow by 2,000,000 in one year. The population and the population density would double in thirty-five years in every nation of the world. Each nation would keep the same percentage of the total population of the world inside its borders.

That's the way it would be if the growth rate were the same everywhere in the world. But it isn't. No, indeed. Just as population density differs from one place to another, so does the growth rate. The 2.0 percent per year figure for the growth rate is the *average* for the world, but it is less in some places and more in others.

In Great Britain, for instance, the growth rate right now is only 0.6 percent per year. Since its population is 56,000,000, this means that the increase of population in Great Britain in the next year will be about 336,000. At this rate, the population of Great Britain will not double until 115 years have passed.

Other nations with growth rates of less than 1 percent are Italy,

Czechoslovakia, Hungary, Belgium, Portugal, Greece, Sweden, Austria, Denmark, Norway and Ireland. East Germany has almost no population increase at all. Its growth rate, right now, is just about zero. Notice that all these low growth rate countries are in the continent of Europe.

The United States and the Soviet Union have growth rates of 1.2 percent per year. This means that the increase in population over the next year will be about 2,500,000 for the United States and about 3,000,000 for the Soviet Union. At this rate, each will double its population in about fifty-eight years.

And what nations have growth rates that are above the world average of 2.0 percent per year?

The largest growth rates in the world, right now, are from 3.5 to 3.7 percent per year. Mexico, for instance, has a growth rate of 3.5 percent per year. Its population is about 53,000,000, and this means that the additional population it will gain this year is 1,850,000. Although Mexico's population is only 1/4 that of the United States, it will add 3/4 as many people to its population over the next year as the United States will.

If the growth rate of 3.5 percent per year were to continue in Mexico, that nation would double its population in only twenty years.

Let's compare the United States with a population of 210,000,000 and a growth rate of 1.2 percent per year and Mexico with a population of 53,000,000 and a growth rate of 3.5 percent per year. If these growth rates were to continue in each nation, then in about sixty years, Mexico will have caught up to the United States in population. Each nation would then have a population of about 420,000,000.

(Such a thing would be true, by the way, only *if* the present growth rates continue. Whenever I say in this book that something will happen *if* the present rate of anything continues, you must always remember that it is very possible that the present rate might *not* continue. In that case, the prediction will not come true.)

Other nations with growth rates in the 3.5 percent neighborhood are the Philippines, Thailand, Colombia, Algeria, Peru, Kenya, Malaysia, Venezuela, Iraq, Ecuador, Guatemala, El Salvador, Honduras, Jordan, Nicaragua, Libya, Costa Rica and Panama. Notice that these are all nations in South America, Africa and Asia. (Of all the continents, South America has the fastest growing population.)

In general, the nations with low population growth rates are industrialized, while the nations with high population growth rates are nonindustrialized.

The industrialized nations have a total population of about 1,200,000,000, nearly 1/3 of the world's population. Their average population growth rate is just under 1.0 percent per year, so that over the next year, they will add about 11,000,000 people to their population.

The nonindustrial nations have a total population of about 2,600,000,000, which is just over 2/3 of the world's population. Their average population growth rate is just under 2.5 percent per year, so that over the next year, they will add about 65,000,000 people to their population.

This means that of the 76,000,000 increase in population this next year, 11,000,000 will be added to the industrialized nations and 65,000,000 (nearly six times as many) to the nonindustrial nations. If this continues year after year, then the nonindustrial nations, which now contain 2/3 of the world's population, will contain 5/6 of the world's population by 2000 A.D.

But this seems rather strange. It doesn't seem to fit the history of the rise in population. When agriculture was developed, the population rise was greatest in the agricultural regions, and that's where the standard of living rose, too. When industrialization took place, the population rise was greatest in the industrial regions, and that's where the standard of living rose, too.

In fact, it seems reasonable to suppose that the population rises rapidly only if the standard of living goes up. Then people are better

WORLD CHILD POPULATION 0-15 YEARS OF AGE

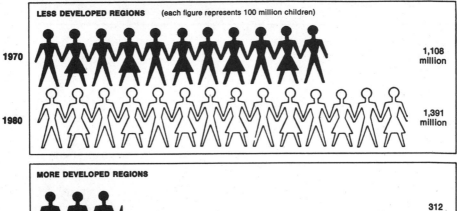

LESS DEVELOPED REGIONS (each figure represents 100 million children)

1970 — 1,108 million

1980 — 1,391 million

MORE DEVELOPED REGIONS

1970 — 312 million

1980 — 331 million

DISTRIBUTION OF WORLD CHILD POPULATION (0-15), 1970
by national per capita income levels $500 or less (each figure represents 50 million children)

$100 AND UNDER — 785 million

$101-300 — 210 million

$301-500 — 75 million

World Child Population 0-15 Years of Age.

fed and more comfortable and secure. They live longer and have more children. The children are better fed and stronger, and more of them live to grow up and have children of their own. The richer a nation is, in other words, the more rapidly we would expect its population to rise.

Yet what is the situation now? Suppose we consider which nations are rich and which are not. One way to do that is to consider the value, in money, of all the goods a nation produces; everything produced by its farms, its mines, its factories. This is its "gross national product," which we can abbreviate as "GNP."

The higher a nation's GNP, the richer you might think it would be. However, there is its population to consider. Suppose we imagine the value of the GNP to be distributed evenly among its entire population. If two nations each have the same GNP and one nation has a population of 1,000,000 while the other has a population of 10,000,000, then there isn't as much value for each person in the larger country. The country with 10,000,000 people has to cut the GNP into more parts, and each person gets only 1/10 as much as the person in the other country gets.

What counts then is "GNP per capita" (that is, per person). The higher the GNP per capita, the richer a country and the higher its average standard of living. (Of course, in some particular country a few powerful people may keep all the value of the GNP for themselves and leave everyone else very poor. Even when this doesn't happen, there are always some who are richer and some who are poorer in every country. We will talk about the average standard of living, however.)

Usually the GNP in each country goes up each year as technology advances and as there are more people to work in the farms, mines and factories. But the population goes up each year, too. If the GNP goes up faster than the population, then the GNP per capita goes up and the nation grows richer. If the population goes up faster than the GNP, then the GNP per capita goes down, and the nation grows poorer.

The highest GNP per capita has, for a number of years, been found in the United States. In 1970, its GNP per capita was $4,760. For that reason, we might say that the United States is the richest country in the world. Sweden is next with $4,040 as its GNP per capita, then Canada with $3,700. In general, industrial nations have a GNP per capita of more than $1,000.

On the other hand, the GNP per capita for Mexico is only $670, for Malaysia only $380, for Thailand only $200, for Uganda only $130, for Afghanistan only $80. In general, nonindustrial nations have a GNP per capital of less than $1,000 and usually less than $500.

There have always been rich nations and poor nations, of course, but the difference has never been as great as it is now. In 1700, when the world was still in the agricultural age, the richest nations had a GNP per capita that was only about five times as high as that of the poorest nations. Today, the richest nations have a GNP per capita that is about sixty times as high as that of the poorest nations.

Yet it is the richest nations that are increasing in population most slowly, and the poorest nations that are increasing most rapidly.

This means that the rich nations can easily increase their GNP faster than their slowly growing population. Their GNP per capita increases and they grow even richer, at least for a while. The poor nations are in a more difficult position. Even though they increase their GNP quite rapidly, their high population growth rate cancels that out. Their GNP per capita stays the same or even decreases and they remain as poor as before.

Why should this be so? Why should the poor regions in the world be increasing in population so much faster than the rich regions? Until now, it has always been the other way around.

Or perhaps we should ask the question the other way around. Why are the industrial nations increasing their population so slowly? If we can answer that question, we might understand more about what makes a growth rate drop and how to prevent the world population from growing past its limits very soon.

In order to answer that question, let's take a closer look at industrialization and see how it has affected population and just exactly how it has changed the growth rate.

7

FOOD

When a nation becomes industrial, it can produce a great many different kinds of manufactured goods in its factories. These factories are powered by steam engines or other devices. Such devices are as powerful as many men and can work longer and more steadily. The existence of these machines multiplies the nation's work force many times.

Yet the machine "workers" do not eat food as human workers do. An industrial nation can trade its manufactured goods abroad for more food than it could grow if all its population were mostly farmers. In addition to that, an industrial nation can build steamships and increase the amount of goods it can move abroad and the amount of food it can bring home.

Great Britain, which was where the first practical steam engine was developed, and which was the first nation to be industrialized, is the best example of this. It, along with other European nations, had already developed overseas colonies, thanks to inventions such as gunpowder and the mariner's compass, which had come before the Industrial Revolution.

Once Great Britain was industrialized, its commerce grew, and it became, for a time, the most powerful nation in the world. Its colonies grew in number and extent. Even though it lost its

American colonies in 1783, Great Britain ended up with the largest empire the world had ever seen. At its peak after World War I, the British Empire included 1/4 of all the land area in the world.

Colonies could be used to supply raw materials for the factories of the ruling nation, and food for the population of the ruling nation. It could be done under conditions that are favorable to the ruling nation. The ruling nation is then better fed and has a higher standard of living.

We can see how this works if we consider Great Britain's population through history. Back in 1100, the population of England alone (which makes up 5/8 of the area of the island of Great Britain) was just under 2,000,000. We know this because of a partial census taken by King William I, in 1086. The population of all of Great Britain may have been 2,500,000 at the time.

Great Britain was only thinly populated then. As the centuries passed, the island was slowly put to greater use in farming and in sheepherding, for instance, so that the population rose slowly.

In 1800, when Great Britain was in the early stages of its industrialization, its population was about 10,000,000. In addition, there were some 4,000,000 people of British descent in the new nation of the United States. That's 14,000,000 people altogether.

In 700 years, the British population had increased 5.6 times. That represents an average growth rate over that period of time of 0.28 percent per year. This meant that the population of Great Britain was doubling (on the average) every 280 years. After 1800, however, as Great Britain grew more and more industrial, the population growth rate was higher, too. What's more, the nations where British immigrants settled in large numbers also grew more industrialized. Their population, too, increased at a very rapid rate.

Now, in 1974, Great Britain has a population of 56,000,000. We can add to that number people of British descent in other industrial nations. We can add the populations of Australia and New Zealand, 2/3 of the population of the United States, half the population of Canada and about 1/12 the population of South Africa. The total comes to 224,000,000.

This means that the British population at home and abroad increased its numbers at an average growth rate of 1.7 percent per year over a period of one and three-quarters centuries. The British population doubled every forty years in that period. This was a much more rapid rise than was true for the rest of the world.

Since 1800, the world's population has increased four times, but the British population at home and abroad has increased sixteen times. In 1800, one person out of every sixty-four in the world was either British or descended from the British. In 1974, this applies to one person out of every seventeen in the world.

This is true also for other industrial nations, though not to the same extent as for Great Britain, which was, after all, the first to become industrial. In 1650, Europe had a population of about 100,000,000 people, or 1/5 the total population of the world. In 1950, people of European origin (who make up most of the population of the industrial nations in Europe itself and on the other continents) numbered 800,000,000—550,000,000 in Europe itself and 250,000,000 on the other continents. This is 1/3 the total population of the world. Europeans increased eight times in population over the last three centuries while non-Europeans increased only three times.

You may see a puzzle here.

Where did all the food come from to feed the growing population of the industrial nations? The machine "workers" do not eat food, but they do not produce food, either, do they? As Great Britain increased in population, it produced less and less food at home and imported more and more food from abroad. So did other industrial nations as their populations increased. Indeed, nowadays 2/3 of the world's population is dependent on imports from regions in which the other 1/3 lives.

But in 1800, before industrialization was more than a mere beginning, the world was producing just about enough food for its population. Where is the food coming from to feed a population four times as high as in 1800?

The answer is that machine "workers" *do* produce food. The machines can be applied to farming also. The steam engine and later power devices can be used to run machinery that could help in farming. Through the 1800s, various mechanical devices were invented that were capable of helping to sow, reap, harvest and so on. One man with machines could plant, care for and harvest crops in as much land, and produce as much food, as five, ten or even twenty men could without machinery.

The United States is the nation where farm machinery was first built and where it was most used. This is what happened. In 1800, the United States had a population of about 5,300,000 people. Of these, 95 percent, or about 5,000,000, worked on farms one way or another. They produced enough food to feed themselves and also to feed the 300,000 who were engaged in commerce and industry. They even produced a surplus to ship abroad in exchange for the foreign goods they needed.

As American farmers began to use more and more machinery, a smaller proportion of the American population had to work on the farms. Nowadays, the number of Americans working on farms represents only 5 percent of the total population. The number of Americans working on farms today is 10,000,000. This is twice as many as

Plowing of a vegetable garden in Matourkou, Africa.
Photo: United Nations

were working on farms in 1800, but the American population has grown forty times. The 10,000,000 work force on American farms today can produce enough food not only for themselves, but also for the 200,000,000 Americans who do not work on farms. In addition, they produce a great deal of food of all kinds that can be sold overseas.

The United States is not only the most industrialized nation in the world, it is the most important food producer as well. This is so *because* it is industrialized. The 10,000,000 farm workers with their machines can do as much work and produce as much food as several hundred million workers without machines. And the machines don't eat the food themselves as the human workers would.

Other nations have industrialized their agriculture, too. What's more, advances in science and technology that have come in industrial nations where more and more people can devote themselves to such things, can be applied to agriculture, and to increasing the food supply.

Dams were built to make sure that certain farming regions always had plenty of water for the crops. Fertilizers were manufactured which made the soil more fertile so that more crops could grow. New methods were worked out for killing or removing other plants or animals that interfered with the growing of crops. This meant that as the number of farm workers decreased, the amount of crops grown on each acre of farmland increased.

Then, too, scientists discovered the importance of vitamins and minerals. They learned the reason why some food which tasted good

Lock-gate in the Sudan helps irrigate the fields.
Photo: United Nations

was nevertheless not very nourishing. They learned what foods one must eat to get the vitamins and minerals necessary to health. They even learned how to manufacture vitamins and add them to food, or put them into pills for people to take. Methods for preserving food were worked out. Food was frozen or canned so it would not spoil. This meant food could be sent long distances more conveniently and without loss.

So, as industrialization proceeded, the food supply of the world went up. It went up much faster than it could possibly have done without industrialization. For instance, one of the reasons that the Netherlands is so densely populated and yet has such a high standard of living is that its farms are so thoroughly fertilized. Full advantage is taken of technological advance, and each acre of farmland in the Netherlands produces four times as much as it would in India, for instance.

All in all, thanks to industrialization, the world's food supply has gone up faster since 1800 than population has. This means that even though the world's population has increased four times since 1800, the average standard of living has gone up, too. It also means that with more food, population has risen everywhere, in nonindustrial nations as well as in industrial nations.

Of course, industrialization has meant a more rapid increase in the industrial nations—in Great Britain, in particular, and in Europe in general. And yet right now, it is the nonindustrial nations that are increasing in population more rapidly than the industrial nations. The reason for that has to be explained, but let's just wait a while for that.

Something else has come up in connection with industrialization. Since industrialization has led to the food supply increasing faster than population for 200 years now, should we assume that this will continue to happen? Are all our worries about population increase needless? Will the food supply continue to increase faster than the population? Will the standard of living continue to go up even though there are more people in the world each year?

Before we can decide that this will indeed happen and that we can stop worrying, we must realize that industrialization has a price. All the machines that work for mankind in the factories, on the farms, in the cities and everywhere else may not eat food themselves, but they do eat something else. They eat "energy."

This means that in considering what is happening in population these days, we must ask what energy is and where it comes from.

Efficient irrigation produces this bountiful harvest near Tel Aviv, Israel. *Photo: United Nations*

8

ENERGY

Anything which has the ability to do work contains energy. Energy comes in many forms. In the outside world, heat, light, sound, electicity, magnetism, motion are all forms of energy. There is also energy in matter, some of which is released when the matter undergoes what is referred to as "chemical changes." This is called "chemical energy."

The most common form of energy about us is the sun's heat and light that fall upon us and upon the whole world. We know the sun's heat and light is a form of energy because it can do work. It can heat the ocean and evaporate it and lift huge quantities of water vapor high into the air.

That water vapor eventually falls as rain. Rain that falls on high ground flows back to the sea in the form of streams and rivers. We know the moving water contains energy because it moves and can push things along with it. Long ago, when people started to build and float rafts downstream, carrying them and their goods, they were using the energy of flowing water that originated from the energy of sunlight.

The sunlight also heats the air. It heats the air unevenly because

the air nearer the equator gets more heat than the air nearer the poles. Because of the uneven heating, there are warm bodies of air on Earth, and cold bodies of air, too. The warm bodies of air rise, and the cold bodies of air sink, resulting in winds all over the world.

The winds contain energy. When people began to put sails on their ships and let the wind blow them across a body of water, they were using the energy of the wind, which originated from the energy of sunlight.

People can use the energy of sunlight directly, too. When they see, they use the energy of sunlight. When they let the warmth of the sun dry their clothes, they use the energy of sunlight.

There are some forms of energy that do not come from the sun. There is heat inside the Earth. In some places, the hot regions appear quite near the surface of the Earth in the form of volcanoes, geysers and hot springs. If a person washes clothes in the water from a hot spring, this "geothermal energy" from the Earth's interior is being used.

Then, too, there are the tides. The water of the ocean rises along the shorelines of the land surface and then falls, and does this twice

Energy from the sun boils water in India. *Photo: United Nations*

each day. The rise and fall is brought about by the turning of the Earth upon its axis. When sailors wait for a high tide to lift their ship and carry it out to sea, they are making use of the Earth's motion.

The most important forms of energy for mankind, however, are various kinds of chemical energy.

To begin with, green plants grow in sunlight (provided they also have water and certain chemicals from the air and the soil). The green plants make use of the energy of sunlight and store it in such places as leaves and stems in the form of certain substances. When these substances are slowly combined with oxygen from the air, a chemical reaction takes place that releases energy. It is on this "chemical energy" that the plant lives, grows and performs all the actions of life.

Plants always store more energy than they are using. Animals can eat the plants, digest them, and change the plant chemicals into their own, which they then store in their own body. In the process about 80 to 90 percent of the energy stored in the plants is lost, and only the remaining 10 to 20 percent is stored in the animal. If the animal eats enough plants, however, he can have all the energy he needs.

When an animal makes use of the stored chemicals in its body and combines them with the oxygen it breathes, it has the energy to enable it to move and perform other functions. The energy of animals' muscles and nerves comes from the energy store of the plants they eat and that comes from the energy of sunlight.

(Energy never comes from nowhere. Whenever and wherever energy exists, it has had to come from somewhere. That is one of the basic rules of the universe.)

Naturally, animals can't eat up all the plants for food, as then there would be nothing left and they would starve. They can only eat that amount of plants which can be replaced by new growth as fast as it is eaten. If animals eat more plants than can be replaced by plant growth, the amount of food they can get grows less. Some animals die of starvation, and that gives the plants a chance to grow to a greater extent than usual because then there are fewer animals to eat them. As the plants grow, there is more food, and the animal population can increase, too.

In this way, there is always a balance or "equilibrium" between plant and animal life. Because animals lose about 85 percent of the plants' food store and save only 15 percent for their own use, the new growth of plant life in the world is always about seven times the new growth of animal life. In other words, it takes about seven kilograms of plant life to support one kilogram of animal life.

Some animals eat other animals. The animal that does the eating loses 85 percent of the stored energy of the animal he eats and saves 15 percent for his own stores. This means that it takes about fifty kilograms of plant life to support seven kilograms of "herbivorous animals" (animals that eat plants) and then one kilogram of "carnivorous animals" (animals that eat other animals).

It is possible to imagine a "food chain." We can imagine an animal that eats another animal that had eaten another animal that had eaten another animal that had eaten a plant. (It always comes down to a plant in the end.) Each step in such a food chain brings about a loss of 80 percent of the energy store. That is why there are more animals that eat plants than there are animals that eat animals that eat plants. The longer the food chain, the smaller the weight of animal that can be supported.

Human beings eat both plants and animals. In fact, human beings can eat such a wide variety of living things that they are said to be "omnivorous" ("eating everything"). On the whole, though, groups of human beings who live on plant food mainly can increase in numbers to a greater extent than groups who live on animal food mainly.

As population density increases, therefore, people must switch in the plant food direction. Land that is used to grow food for human beings can support more people than an equal quantity of land used to grow pasture for animals that are then slaughtered as food for people. The animals have only stored 1/7 the energy available in the plant food, so that if we eat the cattle we get only 1/7 the energy that we would have gotten if we had used the land for plant food we could eat ourselves.

For this reason, animal food is always a luxury. It is more expensive than plant food because it takes more land to produce the animals. In regions with a high standard of living, it is easy to pay the higher prices for animal food, so that a great deal of meat of one sort or another is eaten. In regions with a low standard of living, this is not possible. In nations like India or China, for instance, most people live almost entirely on plant food.

As population increases, it will be harder and harder to produce animal food. It will be more and more necessary to use the land for plant food instead, and more and more of the world will have to turn vegetarian.

For hundreds of thousands of years, the chief energy that people had for their own use was the energy they got from the chemical reactions of their own body. There was also energy from the sun, from wind and running water, from fire—but these were all minor. It was the chemical energy from the food they ate, and then the energy of their own muscles drawn from the food, that did the main work of mankind.

Cattle raising is Paraguay's principal industry. *Photo: United Nations*

The more energy people used, the more likely they were to get enough food and safety. If they moved faster, they could search a larger area for food; if they ran faster, they were more likely to get away from wild animals chasing them; if they dug harder or fought harder, they could collect more plants or kill more animals.

On the other hand, the more energy they used, the more food they needed to replace the energy they lost. If people used twice as much energy to get twice as much food, they didn't make a profit. They had just made themselves more tired for nothing.

What human beings had to do was to use their brains to work out ways of getting back more food for the amount of energy they had to use. One way they could do that was to use energy in such a way as to waste less of it. In other words, energy must be used more efficiently.

For instance, suppose a stone ax is invented. A person's arm would move in the same way and use up just as much energy, but the energy would be concentrated in the hard small tip of the stone head of the ax. It would not be spread over the softer fist. For that reason, the stone ax would deliver a more deadly blow than the fist would. It would kill an animal that a fist would not kill, and a human being would have more food without having to expend more energy.

Other inventions also use energy more efficiently. A bow can throw an arrow much farther than an arm can by concentrating the energy of the arm into the bowstring. Wheels can help move heavy objects over the ground by cutting down the energy waste of friction. A lever can move a heavy object by concentrating into a short distance the energy produced by the arms moving through a long distance.

Another way of making the use of energy more efficient is to cut out the waste involved in looking, hunting and fishing for food. When agriculture came into use, energy had to be used up in planting, plowing, weeding, watering, harvesting and so on. All this was less than the energy used to get a similar amount of food by searching, hunting or fishing. The energy spent in agriculture was much less than the energy that would have been spent in food gathering for the same amount of food.

Most of the technological advance in hundreds of thousands of years of human industry was useful because it put the energy of human muscle to more efficient use. Another way of getting more use out of energy is to get some outside source of energy; something more than is present in the human body itself.

The best source at first was the energy in animal muscle. Some animals that are larger than man can be tamed. Such larger animals have more energy concentrated in their muscles than man has. A donkey, ox, camel or elephant, for instance, can all pull or lift heavier weights than a man can. If they can be trained to do some of man's work for him, more food can be obtained than unaided human beings can produce.

Of course, if an animal were to eat the same food man did, it would make no sense to use him. There would be no profit. The extra food the animal's work helped produce would go to feeding him. Most of the animals tamed by man, however, eat food that man himself cannot eat. An ox, for instance, eats grass, which human beings can't eat, while the work he does—pulling a plow or helping to pump water—grows grain, which human beings can eat.

About the most useful animal in farmwork is the horse. It can pull far harder than a donkey or an ox. Unlike a camel or an elephant, it can work comfortably in cold, wet climates. The trouble is that an animal must be strapped to whatever it is pulling, and the kind of strap arrangement that works for an ox, chokes a horse when he tries to pull.

It wasn't till about 1000 A.D. that the horse collar was invented. About then horseshoes were also invented to protect the horses' tender hooves. It was only after 1000 A.D. that horses could really be used on the farm.

So you see, we can make a general rule. In order to obtain more

An elephant helps clear the land in Ceylon. *Photo: United Nations*

Construction of a dam, in Venezuela, which will produce electricity. *Photo: United Nations*

food, human beings must increase the amount of energy they are using, or they must make use of what energy they do use more efficiently, or both.

More food means a higher population. Therefore, if the human population is to increase without lowering the standard of living, there must be more energy altogether, or more efficient use of energy, or both. If energy runs short and the human population continues to increase, the sure result is that the standard of living will go down. There will be more misery, more starvation.

There is a population explosion when there is a big jump in the energy that people can use. The use of the energy of fire brought the first population explosion. The saving of the use of energy in agriculture, and the use of animal energy that comes with herding brought the second population explosion.

Throughout historical times, up to 1800 A.D., the world population moved up steadily. That was chiefly because agriculture spread over more and more of the world. There were improvements in the efficiency with which energy was used. Bows and arrows were improved, plows were improved and so on, but these were small advances.

There was also the use of outside sources of energy to a larger extent. The energy of wind and running water was used in improved windmills and waterwheels. A new kind of chemical energy was used in gunpowder. Magnetic energy was used in the ship's compass. These were small advances, too.

To get a big advance, one had to develop a big new kind of efficiency or a big new outside source of energy. Until that happened, the way of life could not change very much.

Even in 1800, the fastest a man could travel over land was at the speed of a galloping horse, just as in 2000 B.C. What's more, the tools used in agriculture had changed very little in thousands of years.

But then after 1800 there came the third population explosion, and that had to be the result of a large new source of energy or a really great improvement in efficiency.

What happened?

9

WOOD

Long before the development of agriculture and of herding, people were using a source of energy not produced by their own bodies or by those of living animals.

That source of energy is fire. This is a form of energy produced by chemical reactions outside of living bodies. Chemicals inside the body combine with oxygen in a slow, regular way that produces energy for all the activities of the body. It produces less or more, as you need it, but never very much at one time.

Chemicals outside the body can be made to combine with oxygen quickly, so that a great deal of energy is produced. A bonfire gets much hotter than any animal does. What's more, it pours out so much energy, at such a high temperature, that some of it appears as light.

People might use their own muscles or the muscles of animals as much as they might want, but without fire, they couldn't have done much. Even agriculture wouldn't have helped much. Without fire, they would have had to live in the tropics. Without fire, they could have had no metals, so they would still be making their tools out of stone. They would still be living an almost animal-like existence.

Because people did have fire, however, they had all the benefit

that fire brought. They were able to spread out into colder regions; they could get more food and have more security. It was thanks to the energy of fire added to the energy obtained more efficiently from agriculture and herding than from food hunting that mankind was able to go through two population explosions and reach a population of 900,000,000 in 1800 A.D.

But fire must get its energy from somewhere. It gets it from the combination of some substance with oxygen in the air. A simpler way of putting it is that fire gets its energy from the burning of something. The something that will burn is "fuel."

The most common fuel throughout man's early history was wood. Wood is produced by plants and is chemically very similar to some of the plant substances we use as food. There is just a little chemical difference between the foodstuff and the wood, but that little chemical difference is enough.

The fruits, nuts and seeds of plants—and sometimes the leaves and flowers—are good to eat and supply human beings with considerable energy. The woody parts are useless as food for human beings. If they are eaten, they just pass through the body unchanged.

Pa Parto, of Indonesia, will sell this firewood at the market. *Photo: UNICEF; photographer: Mallica Vajrathon*

No animal can really eat and digest wood. Only certain bacteria can do that. Some animals, such as cattle and termites, have such bacteria in their stomachs and can get more energy out of woody material than we can. Mostly, though, when trees die, their woody parts slowly decay by bacterial action.

For that reason, human beings don't deprive either themselves or their domestic animals of food if they use wood as a fuel. The wood, when it is set on fire, releases energy very quickly, instead of doing it very slowly through bacterial action. By using wood as fuel, no one is cheated except bacteria.

However, once fire made it possible for human beings to increase in numbers, it meant that more and more fire was needed. There were more people who needed to be warmed, more people who needed light. More of the things fire produced were needed; more metals, more glass, more pottery, more cooked food. Too, more and more wood was needed to build more and more houses and make more and more furniture and other objects for the more and more people in the world.

As time went on, the forests began to disappear in those places where the population increased most. The trees were chopped down to be used for fuel and for other reasons. It didn't seem to matter, as one could always get wood from other regions where the population was still low. Of course, with every century, forests were destroyed more and more quickly. When European colonists arrived in North America in the 1600s, vast stretches of the continent were covered with forest. Now, much of it is gone.

This is an example of how people use up "resources," the raw material they need for their activities. The greater the number of people, the more quickly the resources are used up.

In the case of the forests, it was not just a matter of trees. All the different kinds of plants and animals have lives that are interconnected. Trees, for instance, are homes for birds, food for insects and so on. What's more, the different kinds of plants and animals are interconnected with the Earth itself. The trees have roots which trap water and keep it from flowing away too fast so that the soil stays moist. Trees have leaves that give off water and give shade below, and this helps keep the climate a little cooler than it would otherwise be.

When trees are gone, water flows through the soil more quickly, carrying the soil away. What soil is left behind is drier and less fertile; and the climate is warmer.

For these reasons, many of the regions where mankind first increased in numbers have climates that are worse now than they used to be a few thousand years ago. Partly, this is because of the activities of people. By cutting down the trees faster than they could grow again, they upset the balance among the different kinds of living things and between them and the Earth itself. The balance can be kept through the slow changes in the Earth and in living things over many tens of millions of years. It couldn't be kept when mankind introduced changes in mere thousands of years, then in mere hundreds of years.

The interconnectedness of living things among themselves and with the Earth is called the "ecology." When people introduced big changes quickly, they upset the ecology. The larger the number of people, the greater the changes they are likely to make, and the shorter the time in which they make them. Therefore, the extent to which they are likely to upset the ecology gets larger as population density increases.

Almost everything people do upsets the ecology, often to their own harm. For that reason, people must always consider whether the upset is worth the accomplishments they are trying to carry through.

Consider agriculture, for instance——

A tract of land which is not being farmed is likely to have a large variety of different plants growing on it. Living there, also, is a large variety of different animals, each living on certain plants (or on each other) in certain ways. Once agriculture is introduced, the entire tract of land is given over to just a few kinds of plants that are useful to people. Other kinds of plants are called "weeds" and are killed off.

This means that animals that can't live on the kind of plants that are being grown must leave the area or die off. On the other hand, animals that *can* live on the kind of plants being grown have a much greater food supply than they would ever have had if people were not engaging in agriculture. What's more, all the food supply is conveniently in one place. For that reason, those animals increase in numbers just as human beings do. Crows, rats and locusts can multiply to very great crowds sometimes.

Then, too, as people multiply in numbers, thanks to agriculture, and live close together in cities, all kinds of waste products form in this small area. There are leftover food ("garbage") and human wastes, and the smoke and smell of fire. All these wastes that are formed in quantities greater than can be disposed of are examples of "pollution."

As people increase in number, so does pollution. Some very ancient cities in the Middle East have long ago disappeared but have left behind the mounds of garbage and other wastes that had gradually accumulated about them.

Then, too, as human beings come to live close together, in greater and greater numbers, and as wastes accumulate, bacteria that live in human beings and on those wastes also increase in number. It becomes easier for those bacteria to pass from human being to human being as the distance between human beings grow less. Some of the bacteria cause disease so, as the human population increases and crowds together, fast-spreading sicknesses ("epidemics") become more common.

The advantage of having more food made agriculture worthwhile even though there were the disadvantages of animal pests, pollution and disease.

Then, too, the disadvantages were most serious in the places where population density was high, and until recently those places were few. Forests disappeared, soil grew less fertile and there were

New York City produces over 24,000 tons of garbage a day. *Photo: United Nations*

These villagers are plowing their field. *Photo: UNICEF*

other manmade difficulties in the Middle East and in other places where there were high population densities, but the great mass of land on Earth remained untouched.

Even as late as the 1700s, most of the Earth's surface was in more or less its original state. The continuing increase in human population still had not done too much damage to the ecology.

During all that time, right through the 1700s, wood remained the chief fuel of mankind. There were other fuels, too. There was animal fat or beeswax which could be used to make candles. There were oils of various kinds that could be used in lamps. These fuels were used only in a small way.

And, right through the 1770s, fire was used for much the same purposes it had been used through all the centuries. It heated houses, gave light, cooked food and helped make metal, glass, pottery and so on.

The energy of fire was never used to do the kind of work that the energy of muscles did. Despite the thousands of years of the use of fire; despite the use of wind and running water; despite the use of the chemical energy of gunpowder and the magnetic energy of the compass, most of the labor needs of mankind were carried through by the energy of muscles. Right into the 1700s, almost all the heaving, pushing, pulling, twisting, straining that went into mankind's work was done by the muscles of man and his domestic animals.

And then came the steam engine, and everything changed.

10

COAL

Suppose fire were used to heat water. The water would be turned into steam which would then take up a lot more room than the original water would. If the water were heated in a closed container, the steam—trying to take up more room—would push against the walls with great force. If there were a hole in the wall of the container, the steam would come whistling out with great force. The energy of the escaping steam could then be put to work.

Even some ancient Greeks knew of the energy of steam, but they never built any devices that would make good use of it. For one thing, in order to build such devices, some very clever and complicated work had to be done. Everything had to fit together very well and be airtight or the steam would escape in the wrong way. Also, the water would have to be heated and the steam cooled again with as little waste as possible. Finally, the energy of the escaping steam would have to be directed so that it would push and pull rods in such a way that the rods would, in turn, turn wheels.

A device which uses steam to push rods and turn wheels is a "steam engine." As I said earlier in the book, the first really practical steam engine was built by a Scottish engineer named James Watt, in 1769. For the first time, mankind had a "prime mover" that used

heat, an engine that took heat energy from a nonliving source and made it do the muscle work of mankind. It was this steam engine that began the Industrial Revolution.

In the 1830s, it was discovered that if a metal object was kept turning between the poles of a magnet, an electric current could be produced. It took work to keep the metal object turning, but a steam engine could be made to do that work. Electric currents began to be produced in greater and greater quantity. The electric currents could make wheels turn in "motors," and in the late 1800s more and more of man's work was done by electricity.

As steam engines multiplied, fuel was used to a larger and larger extent, and population continued to grow, thanks to the production of more and more energy.

But *what* fuel?

Even in the late 1700s, the forests of the Earth were still enormous, and wood was still available in large quantities. Yet to satisfy man's growing use of energy, those forests would have had to be cut down. That would have made steam engines too expensive to use, as man has great need of forests for other purposes than just to burn them up. In Great Britain, where the steam engines first began to multi-

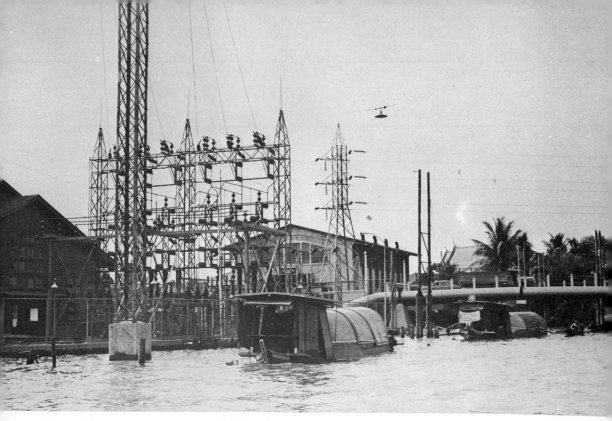

Electricity is distributed from this power plant in Thailand. *Photo: United Nations*

ply, the forests were already mostly gone, anyway. Fortunately, there was another fuel available in Great Britain, and that was coal.

Coal is a leftover remnant of long-dead forests of the past. About 350 million years ago, the temperature of the Earth was mild. The continents were low-lying swampy plains, with shallow inlets of the ocean here and there. The moist warmth resulted in the vast growth of primitive trees.

When such trees died, they fell into the shallow water. There they decayed in such a way that some parts of the chemicals in them were changed into water and gases. Other parts were left behind in solid form. What was left behind in solid form was coal, which is made up largely of an element called "carbon." The coal was covered over by rock and soil, as time passed, and after hundreds of millions of years, large quantities of coal existed in layers under the ground, here and there on the Earth.

Coal does not burn in the same way that wood does. When wood is heated some of its substances break away as gases. These gases burn easily and give off heat and light. When coal is heated, there is much less gas given off. That means coal is harder to set on fire, burns more slowly and gives off less light. It gives more heat, however, and lasts longer.

Coal, then, is wood of the long, long past. Since remains of life of the long, long past are called "fossils," coal is an example of a "fossil fuel."

There is an important difference between wood and coal. New wood grows each year in quite large quantities. Coal is formed so slowly, however, that we might as well consider that no new coal is being formed. If we use wood only in the amount that is replaced by growing trees, then our fuel supply would last forever. Wood is a "renewable fuel." The trouble is that if we use only that amount of wood, there won't be enough fuel for man's needs.

Coal being mined in Belgium. *Photo: United Nations/ILO*

Industry contributes to air pollution in the Federal Republic of Germany. *Photo: United Nations*

We can use coal in much greater quantity since it doesn't do us any good while it is in the ground, so that it seems we might as well burn it and get some good out of it. Of course, eventually the coal would be used up, but that appeared to be a pretty long "eventually." There seemed endless quantities of coal underground.

By 1900, coal had replaced wood as the chief fuel in all the industrialized nations. In fact, about 96 percent of man's energy needs were being derived from burning coal. By then, mankind was burning nearly a billion tons of coal each year, but even at that rate, there seemed enough coal underground to last for thousands of years.

It was because of the energy of burning coal that the world's population was able to increase from 900,000,000 to 1,600,000,000 between 1800 and 1900, while the average standard of living also rose.

To be sure, all that coal burning produced a great deal of smoke and soot. Those cities where industries of all kinds existed—such as Pittsburgh in the United States, and Birmingham in Great Britain—became soot-caked, dirty and dingy. That was considered a sign of prosperity, though. Even in 1900, there wasn't enough pollution produced by burning coal to affect the whole world much.

Yet, coal had its disadvantages. Getting it out of the ground was a dirty, difficult and dangerous job. Once it was out of the ground, shipping it to factories here and there was a big job, too. As the world used more and more coal year after year, there had to be more and more coal miners digging out more and more coal, and more and more railroad cars were needed to carry the coal.

What made coal so difficult to handle was that it was solid. There is, however, another fossil fuel that is liquid and was much, much easier to handle than coal was. It is called "petroleum" or, more simply "oil."

11

OIL

Oil, like coal, formed many ages ago. It may have formed from tiny sea creatures which died and were buried in the ooze of shallow sea bottoms. The fatty parts of the cells of these creatures collected and, over the years, changed into oil.

Oil contains carbon, as coal does. It also contains hydrogen. The carbon and hydrogen, combined together, form very tiny collections of atoms called "molecules." Because only hydrogen and carbon are present in the molecules, they are know as "hydrocarbon molecules." Oil is a mixture of hydrocarbon molecules of various sizes. The larger the molecule, the more sludgy the hydrocarbon is, and the harder it is to heat it and make a gas of it.

In oil, there are very big molecules that produce a kind of tar when separated out. There are smaller molecules which produce a thick liquid that doesn't evaporate much when it is heated. There are still smaller molecules which produce a thinner liquid that evaporates easily when it is heated, and it then becomes a gas. And there are very small molecules that bubble off as "natural gas" at once, even when it is cold.

All these different kinds of hydrocarbons have their uses and all can burn. The smaller the molecule, the more easily it can burn.

When oil is treated in such a way that the different kinds of hydro-carbon are separated, each for its own use, the oil is "refined."

Oil is lighter than water, so it slowly makes its way up through the water in the soil and through tiny cracks and holes in rock. Sometimes the oil reaches the surface and collects there as a kind of sticky, thick, black liquid. Even ancient man knew about oil that reaches the surface in that way. He made use of it sometimes.

Most oil, however, rose upward till it reached a layer of solid rock with no tiny holes in it. Then it could rise no further and just stayed there. If a hole was bored through that solid rock, oil from the trapped pool would shoot up to the surface. This was an "oil well."

The first person to "drill" for oil in this way was Edwin Drake. He drilled an oil well in Titusville, Pennsylvania, in 1859.

Once an oil well is located, the oil is much easier to handle than coal is. No one has to go deep underground in order to chip out solid chunks of material. A hole is drilled, and the oil then comes up by itself. Instead of having to carry it here and there by railroad, oil can pour through pipes to wherever you want it to go. (If you want to send oil overseas, however, you have to use big ships called "tankers.")

The biggest difficulty in dealing with oil is finding those places where there are pools of oil underground. People didn't try very hard to do this at first, because there didn't seem to be many uses for oil. In the second half of the 1800s, oil was used mostly for lighting. Oil was slowly burned in special lamps. Usually it was some sort of animal oil that was used. In the early 1800s, men hunted whales and used "whale oil" for lamps.

It was easier to get oil from the ground, though, and separate the molecules that formed a liquid called "kerosene." Kerosene lamps became quite popular.

Then, toward the end of the 1800s, engines were designed which were run by liquid fuel. Instead of setting up a steam engine outside and using the steam to push rods and turn wheels, a liquid hydrocarbon was used inside the engine. This liquid was a fraction of oil which evaporated very easily and was called "gasoline." A little bit of the gasoline was evaporated, and the vapor was sent into the engine. There it combined with oxygen rapidly in a kind of explosion. The force of the explosion set rods moving and wheels to

turning and made a wagon go by itself without a horse pulling it. In this way, the "automobile" was invented.

A motor which is powered by explosions inside itself is an "internal-combustion engine." In many ways, it is more convenient than the steam engine. In a steam engine you must wait for the water to heat and for the steam to form. Gasoline evaporates so easily, even on cold days, that the internal-combustion engine can start at once.

As the automobile was improved, it became more and more popular. There were more and more automobiles on the streets of the cities of industrial nations and that meant that more and more gasoline had to be used. People began to look for oil wells and learned how to recognize the kind of regions in which they were to be found.

Other parts of the oil were used, too. "Diesel fuel" was made up of molecules bigger than those of gasoline and it was used in trucks, buses, locomotives and ships. "Fuel oil" was made of still heavier molecules and it was used to heat buildings and to run the generators that produced electricity. The very small molecules of natural

An oil refinery and storage tanks in Saudi Arabia. *Photo: UNATIONS/ARAMCO*

Farmer uses a diesel pump to irrigate his fields in India. Photo: *UNICEF; photographer: Trevor Drieberg*

gas were also used to heat buildings and to cook food. In addition, the hydrocarbon molecules of oil were to make all sorts of new products such as plastics, dyes and medicines.

Throughout the 1900s, the use of oil in one form or another rose steadily. Even though the use of coal continued to go up in the 1900s, it didn't go up as fast as it did in the 1800s. Oil gained on it. By 1935, oil had caught up in the United States, at least, and it kept going higher still. Nor did there seem to be any need to hold back in using oil. After World War II, very rich regions of oil were found in the Middle East, and it became cheaper than ever. Oil was produced and used in greater and greater quantities, not only in the United States, but in all the industrial nations.

By the 1970s, the United States was using four times as much oil as coal. This same sort of thing was happening all over the world. Even though the world was using three billion tons of coal per year— over three times as much as in 1900—oil was far outstripping it. It was the huge quantity of energy obtained from oil—in a very convenient and cheap way—that made it possible for the world's population to more than double since 1900 and for there still to be a rising standard of living.

Of course, there are disadvantages to using more and more fossil fuel. The total amount of coal and oil being burned now is about ten times what it was in 1900. That means that much more air pollution is being produced than in 1900. There is enough pollution now to make the air all over the world a little dirtier than it used to be. Nor is it just the air which grows dirtier. As the use of energy goes up, factories and industries spread out over the face of the world. They produce all kinds of wastes, some of which are poisonous.

These wastes are usually flushed away by water, so that the poisons get into the soil, into lakes and rivers and, finally, into the ocean. Some of the oil that is carried over the ocean in tankers also gets into the ocean. What this means is that the soil and water of the world are getting dirtier and are slowly being poisoned.

Some wastes are solid and don't get into the soil or water. As the standard of living goes up and as more is bought and more is used, more and more is thrown away. There is a mountain of solid waste:

Iraq's oil resources are of great importance to its economy. *Photo: United Nations*

more garbage, more paper, more cans, more bottles, more everything. It is harder and harder to find places to put all this waste.

It is up to scientists and engineers to find a way to stop this pollution if they can, but what makes this hard is the *way* in which population is rising. Increasing use of energy makes it possible for population to go up, and as population goes up there is always the demand for more energy—which makes pollution go up still further—and makes the need for still more energy ——

This is called a "vicious cycle."

One problem is this. We can't say that the standard of living is high enough, and that we ought to be satisfied at the level we now have. Unfortunately, not everyone in the world enjoys a really high standard of living. The kind of high standard of living that comes with the use of a great deal of energy is found mostly in the industrial nations and particularly in the United States.

The United States has 1/18 of the world's population, but it uses 1/3 of the world's supply of energy each year. This means that the average American uses six times as much energy as the average non-American.

Most of the rest of the world's energy is used by the other industrial nations. In fact, it is estimated that the average person in the industrial nations—including the United States, the Soviet Union, Japan and western Europe—uses eighteen times as much energy as the average person in the nonindustrial areas.

Since the nonindustrial areas are increasing in population much faster than the industrial areas, this difference between the people who use a lot of energy and the people who use only a little energy is getting worse each year. The difference in standard of living between rich nations and poor nations is greater than it has ever been before in history, and it is worse for another reason as well ——

In the past, people in one part of the earth didn't know anything at all about people in another. People who were living in very primitive conditions in Italy in 3000 B.C. didn't know that Egypt was a land

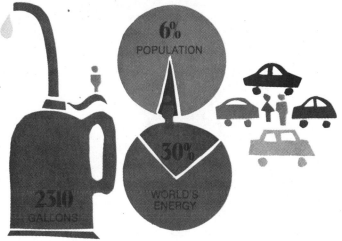

Americans are energy gluttons

We have 6% of earth's population but consume 30% of total energy. Each year we have a net gain of 2 million people — but add 4 million cars.

6%
POPULATION

30%

WORLD'S
ENERGY

2310
GALLONS

Americans consume 30 percent of the Earth's energy.

of rich temples and plentiful food. If they *had* known, their own life might have seemed much more miserable in comparison.

Now, in the present, for the first time, everyone knows about everyone else. Thanks to the development of science and industry, such things as movies and television have spread over the world. It has also become easy for people to travel and see other parts of the world. People in nonindustrial areas, with a very low standard of living, can see for themselves how well-off people are elsewhere every time they watch television or go to the movies. They can see how well tourists live.

In fact, even in the various industrial nations, there are groups of people who are not well-off and who can see how other, wealthier groups are living. As a result of all this, there is a great demand for a higher standard of living among all peoples. It is, therefore, very difficult to take the attitude that we must limit the use of energy in order to give us a chance to take care of pollution. Instead,

This station will supply power to the industry in India's Damodar Valley.
Photo: United Nations

there is a great demand to use more and more energy so that poor nations, and poor people in rich nations, can share in the high standard of living.

Since World War II, the rate of use of energy has been increasing far more rapidly than the population; the quantity of energy used has been doubling every fifteen years.

This might look good. By the time the world population has doubled, the amount of energy used will have increased four times. If that were to go on, then by about 2025 A.D. the energy used by each person in the world will, *on the average,* be equal to that of the energy used by each person in the United States, on the average, today.

If that were so, and if we imagined all that energy distributed among the nations a little more evenly than it is today, we might then decide that the world had reached a high enough standard of living. We could call a halt and begin to concentrate chiefly on pollution.

But can we? There are two catches.

One of them is that population is likely to continue rising. If it does, the use of energy must rise also to match that. We can't just call a halt or the standard of living will go down as more people are added to the world's population.

The second catch is that a crisis will come in our use of energy long before 2025. In fact, the crisis is coming now, in the 1970s ——

12

CRISIS

Right now, the world is getting over 90 percent of its energy from the fossil fuels, oil and coal. We are using more and more of fossil fuels each year. We have used up more fossil fuel in the years since World War II than in all the history of mankind before.

How long can we keep on using those fossil fuels before running out of them? In particular, how long can we keep on using them if we keep on doubling the amount we use every fifteen years? Scientists can estimate how much fossil fuel there is in the Earth right now. There is enough to last us at the present rate of use for perhaps 7,500 years.

That, however, is only if it can all be gotten out of the ground. Some of it is so deeply buried, or is spread out so thinly, that it would take more energy to get it out, than the energy we would get back from it once we had it. We would actually lose energy instead of getting it.

If we count only the amount of fossil fuel we could get out of the ground in such a way as to get more energy than we spend, we might have enough to last us only for 1,000 years.

At least, it will last us 1,000 years if we just use it at the present rate. If we keep doubling the rate of use every fifteen years, the fossil fuel supply will only last perhaps 135 years.

Of course, people might argue that we *won't* be doubling the rate of energy use forever. Eventually, we will level off. But not if population keeps going up. Maybe we could squeeze more than 135 years out of the fossil fuels if population keeps going up, but these fuels will certainly be used up in far less than 1,000 years.

And that means both coal and oil. It is oil that is much the more convenient of the two and it is oil that is being turned to more and more. And oil, it so happens, is in much shorter supply than coal is.

The amount of oil in oil wells is going to run out, at the present rate of use, in only thirty to, at most, fifty years. If we keep on using it at a greater and greater rate, as we have been doing, it will be gone in twenty years. Another problem in connection with oil is that it is not spread out over the world as well as coal is. As long as coal was the chief fuel, industrial nations like Great Britain and Germany had enough fuel on their own territories to power their industries.

Where oil is concerned, many of the industrial nations have almost none on their own territories. Japan and the nations of western Europe do not have oil and must get it from abroad. In fact, the only industrial nations that have large quantities of oil of their own are the United States and the Soviet Union.

The United States, however, is one of the most industrialized nations, and it uses far more oil than any other nation. In the last thirty years, it has increased its uses of oil so much that it no longer produces enough oil for itself.

About 3/5 of the oil supply of the world is found in the Middle East, in such nations as Libya, Saudi Arabia and Iran. The nation of Kuwait, on the Persian Gulf, with an area only 3/4 that of the small American state of Massachusetts, and with a population of only about half a million, has twice as much oil as all the United States has.

This means that a great deal of money is shifting from the industrial nations, who need the oil and can't do without it, to the oil-producing nations which can charge almost any price they want. As a result, Kuwait, which not very many years ago was a barren waste on which people lived primitive lives, had a GNP per capita of $3,760 in 1970. That figure is still going up, and soon Kuwait may be the richest nation in the world.

This wealth is not the result of industrialization, but entirely because of the oil Kuwait sells. Other formerly poor nations, like Libya and Saudi Arabia, are now rich and are rapidly growing richer because of the oil they possess. This has placed the industrial nations of the world in a very shaky position. They must depend on the goodwill of the oil-producing nations.

In 1973, because of troubles in the Middle East, the oil-producing nations decided to limit their sales of oil. Suddenly, the industrial nations, which for so many years had been used to living well, found they had to cut down on automobile use, limit the heating of houses, slow down their factories.

Everyone began to speak of an "energy crisis."

To some people it might have seemed that the energy crisis would only last for a little while. They felt that the oil-producing nations would soon change their minds and let the industrial nations buy oil. Eventually, they did indeed do so, but at a much higher price. Besides, if things keep on as they have, all the oil wells will begin to go dry in about twenty years.

Automobiles are a major source of Tokyo's air pollution. *Photo: United Nations*

Between higher prices and dwindling supplies, the energy crisis will be permanent. Or, at least, it will be if we depend on oil as our chief source of energy.

There are, of course, other sources of energy. Even if oil runs low, we can go back to coal, which will last much longer. This won't be easy. Coal is hard to get out of the ground, and to move from place to place. What's more, you can't run automobiles and airplanes on coal. Mankind switched from coal to oil because oil was so much more suitable as an energy source. To switch back will be hard.

Of course, it is possible to treat coal at the mines in such a way as to convert it into a kind of an oil. Then it is this oil that can be shipped and used. Such oil, made from coal, would be far more expensive than the oil we get from wells. It is also possible to get oil

Users ahead of explorers

Known reserves of many key minerals will be depleted in two or three decades at today's rates of consumption. That is, unless science and technology make new breakthroughs — and explorers keep up with consumers.

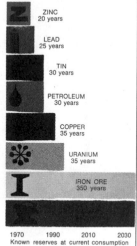

ZINC
20 years

LEAD
25 years

TIN
30 years

PETROLEUM
30 years

COPPER
35 years

URANIUM
35 years

IRON ORE
350 years

1970   1990   2010   2030
Known reserves at current consumption

Natural gas crisis

Known natural gas reserves will last only 13 years. Use is up 300% since 1950. Experts see rationing by 1976.

Reserves are shrinking

TRILLION CUBIC FEET
13.8
Used 1971

New discoveries
6.4

1970 Consumption

Where we get our energy

Big switch from coal to petroleum products will probably have to swing back to coal. Nuclear energy expanding fast — but not fast enough.

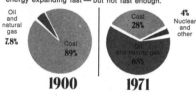

Oil and natural gas
7.8%

Coal
89%

1900

Coal
28%

Oil and natural gas
68%

4%
Nuclear and other

1971

Our energy resources are being depleted quickly.

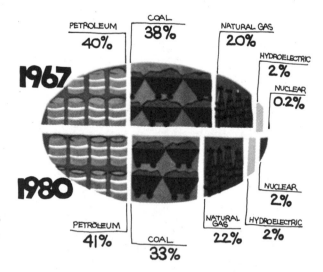

PETROLEUM
40%

COAL
38%

NATURAL GAS
20%

HYDROELECTRIC
2%

NUCLEAR
0.2%

1967

1980

PETROLEUM
41%

COAL
33%

NATURAL GAS
22%

NUCLEAR
2%

HYDROELECTRIC
2%

Fossil fuel will continue to supply our energy needs — until it is gone.

1. World sources of energy

Oil will continue to be No. 1 for many years . . . *Coal* is losing ground, but with five trillion tons reserve is good intermediate-term bet . . . *Nuclear energy* with most long-term promise, is being developed very slowly. So fossil fuel — a non-renewable resource and biggest air polluter — will supply world's energy for decades to come.

out of certain kinds of rock called "shale." This is very common in some parts of the world, and the oil supply in shale is great. Such oil would also be far more expensive than oil from wells.

Besides that, to dig out the coal or the shale in great enough quantities to run the world's industries, even at just the present level, would do great harm to the environment. And finally, the fossil fuel of all kinds *will* run out in a few hundred years at most, if the population keeps going up as it has been. If people depend on fossil fuels for energy and nothing else, mankind faces a crisis much more dangerous than any he has ever faced before.

Suppose people had slowly increased their numbers when they were living in a food-gathering way of life, and reached the point where the food supply would support no more of them. There wouldn't be quite enough plants and animals to supply the whole human population, but those plants and animals wouldn't disappear entirely. There would still be some. Some people would starve to death, but most people would manage to live.

Or suppose people had more rapidly increased their numbers while they were living an agricultural way of life and reached the point where the food supply would support no more of them. There wouldn't be quite enough food produced by the world's farms, but there would still be a great deal. The farms wouldn't all disappear. Some people would starve, but most people would manage to live.

This time it's different. People are very rapidly increasing their numbers while living an industrial way of life. But industries do not depend on plants and animals in the wild which won't disappear. They do not depend on farms and herds which won't disappear. They depend on the energy of fossil fuel, which *will* disappear.

If the fossil fuels are used up, and there is nothing to take their place, then industry would collapse. There would then be billions of people in the world that a nonindustrial world could not support. It would be as though the world population had gone up and up and up—and had then gone over a cliff.

The Tequendama Falls in Colombia may one day supply electricity. *Photo: United Nations*

And yet fossil fuels are not all there is. They are our major present source of energy, but they are *not* the only source of energy. Perhaps, then, the human race can save itself from catastrophe.

There are energy sources that people have been using all through history—including the wind, the tides and running water. This kind of energy doesn't produce pollution. Nor will it run out as long as the sun shines and the Earth turns. There isn't enough of this kind of energy to operate all the world's industries, but it can help out, and that's important, too.

There is the energy from the heat inside the Earth and from sunlight. Scientists and engineers are trying to work out methods for making use of such energy, and, eventually, we ought to be able to use it in great quantity. And such energy will last as long as the Earth and sun stay in their present condition.

There is also "nuclear energy"—energy from deep inside the center of the atoms that make up everything about us. There are already power plants that make use of the energy of "nuclear fission." More and more energy could be supplied in this fashion. The trouble with this is that it makes use of a rather rare metal called "uranium," which produces a particularly dangerous kind of pollution.

A more hopeful energy source of this kind is "nuclear fusion." It makes use of common substances such as hydrogen; it produces far more energy than nuclear fission does; and it is certain to be far safer. The trouble is that scientists have not yet figured out the details of making fusion work.

So you see, there is a great deal of energy that mankind could use, even if the fossil fuels run out. There is energy that will last as long as mankind does.

But some of these energy sources are not large enough for our needs, some are a little too dangerous, and some have not yet been worked out in detail. It will take time for scientists and engineers to work out the necessary details and to make it possible for mankind to switch from fossil fuels to other energy sources in such a way that the other energy sources will be sufficient to power the world's industries.

In India, atomic research may solve serious problems of drought, food wastage and energy shortages. *Photo: United Nations*

We can't predict how long it will take to make the switch. The sensible thing to do would be to use as little oil and coal as possible. That would stretch out the fossil fuel supply and give us more time.

But suppose population increases while we are waiting for the complete switch from fossil fuel energy to energy from other sources. The higher the population, the greater the pressure to use more energy. If the population increases and the rate of energy use stays the same, then the amount of energy used per person goes down and the standard of living goes down, too.

Naturally, people aren't going to want to have their standard of living go down. They aren't going to want to go hungry. So there will be the push to use more and more energy, and there will be less time to make the switchover. What's more, by the time scientists and engineers have devised ways of getting enough energy from other sources to run the world of the 1970s, the amount of energy being used may have risen beyond that.

It could then be that the switchover can never be made. It could be that the ability of the new sources to supply energy will fall further and further behind the needs of a constantly growing population. It might be like trying to catch someone who can run faster than you can.

Some people might think that it is just a matter of rationing energy and letting the standard of living fall. If many people starve and die, they may think, that will bring the population down again. Then, when the new sources of energy are plugged in, we can move ahead again. It would be too bad that so many people would die, but that might seem the price we would have to pay.

That is a pretty unpleasant way of looking at the future, and it might not work, either.

One thing that the industrialization of the world has meant has been the growth of cities. Industrialization has meant that fewer and fewer people are needed to run the farms. It also means that there are more and more factories and offices grouped about the cities, and factories and offices mean jobs. People, therefore, move from the farms to the cities, looking for work that will help them earn a living.

In the industrial nations nowadays, about 64 percent of the population live in and around the cities. The percentage is as high as 80 percent in nations such as Belgium and Sweden. The people in and around cities make up an "urban population," and the total number in the industrial nations is 750,000,000.

Only about 25 percent of the people in nonindustrial nations are urban; that is, about 650,000,000. The percentage is lowest in Africa, where it is only 11 percent. In the world today, then, a total of 1,400,000,000 people are urban, while 2,400,000,000 live in country areas and are "rural."

The movement toward the cities continues, and the urban population is increasing at a far faster rate than the rural population is. Right now, 3/8 of the world's population is urban. By 2005, when the world's population will have doubled, at least 1/2 will be urban. The rural population will have increased to about 3,500,000,000, which is 1.5 times what it is now, but the urban population will have increased to about 3,500,000,000 also, 2.5 times what it is now. Most of the new growth in urban population will be in nonindustrial nations.

It is very unlikely that the cities will be able to give the larger populations the same kind of food, houses and services that they now supply. At present, the service supplied by most cities is not very good and it is bound to get worse as more people crowd in.

More and more people will have to live in shacks or in streets or in "shantytowns" around the city itself. There have been estimates that by 2000 A.D., 3/4 of the urban population—2,700,000,000—will be living in shantytown slums.

As the cities get more and more crowded, and, in particular, as the slums get more and more crowded, there is more misery, more unrest, more crime. Just the effort to correct this will place more and more of a strain on each nation and on the world.

It could be that we can't just say "Let enough people starve and

that will bring down the population." People don't want to starve, and as billions struggle for food, they may bring down the structure of civilization with them.

You see then why I have spent five chapters talking about energy.

It turns out that we simply will not avoid disaster within a few decades if population keeps going up and up. We must find some way of stopping that population.

There is this hope—population growth *has* slowed in some places.

Remember that at the end of Chapter 6, we asked why it was that the population of the industrial nations was growing so slowly. In the 1800s, it had been the industrial nations that had grown most rapidly in population. In the middle 1900s, however, they grew very slowly, while the nonindustrial nations were growing rapidly.

If we knew what had happened to slow down the growth rate of the industrial nations, we might get an idea of what must be done to slow down the growth rate of the nonindustrial nations. Then the world might have a chance.

Well, then, what happened?

Two alternatives to housing shortages—shanties or modern apartments. *Photo: WHO*

13

BIRTH RATE

Suppose we look once again at how population changes ——

There are two forces that change the population. There is the rate at which people die (the death rate) and the rate at which they are born (the birth rate).

It is quite easy for a society to have a high birth rate. Babies are born as a result of the mating between men and women, and most men and women enjoy mating. If there is a great deal of mating, as there often seems to be, there are a great many babies born.

As a result, a society may well have a birth rate of 50 per thousand per year, or even more. Thus, the birth rate in Swaziland today is 52.3 per thousand per year.

With a birth rate of 50 per thousand per year, there will be 1,050 people at the end of the year for every 1,000 people at the beginning. If no one died, that would be a growth rate of 5 percent per year and the population would double in twelve years.

But people do die. In a nonindustrial region it is even possible for the death rate to be very high. If there is no modern medicine to keep down disease and to improve diet, and if there is no great supply of food to keep people from starving, it is even possible for the death rate to be about 50 per thousand per year.

Despite very high birth rates, then, the population of primitive societies rises slowly, if at all. The very high death rate takes care of that.

As a society becomes more complex, the death rate goes down somewhat even if no industrialization takes place. There may be no modern medicine, but there would be more food and better protection against death by violence.

What often happens in that case is that the birth rate goes down somewhat, too. Rules are established for marriage, and mating is not something that anyone can do at anytime he or she wants to.

In Great Britain about 1650, for instance, the birth rate was down to about 35 per thousand per year, and so was the death rate. The death rate was a little lower than the birth rate (as it usually is) so that there was a slow increase in population. The increase was faster than in earlier times but it was still slow.

Considering the high death rate, it has always seemed necessary for people to have many children. Without that, it seemed quite clear, population would dwindle and a society would die out. There seemed other reasons, too, why it was useful to have children.

In a nonindustrial society, most people work on farms, and

Infant mortality is an ever-present problem in Mexico. *Photo: UNICEF; photographer: John Weisblat*

children quickly grow big enough to help with the chores. Grownups without children would not have this help and taking care of the farm would be harder for them.

Furthermore, in a nonindustrial society, there is usually no help for people who are sick and old except from other members of the family. Children will support their parents, and people who do not have children may face an old age in which they will die with no one to help them.

For these reasons, many children were a blessing. Fathers felt that having children showed what powerful and strong men they were. Mothers felt that having children showed what real women they were. Lack of children, on the other hand, seemed like a cruel misfortune; like a curse.

What happens, though, when a nation becomes industrialized? The death rate starts dropping. As more energy is put to use, the food supply goes up. As science develops, disease becomes less deadly.

The birth rate, however, stays high at first, because people are used to having many children and considering it right and proper to have many children. In the first stages of industrialization, then, there is a very large population growth rate. It was in this way that Great Britain increased its population so rapidly in the 1800s. The death rate fell, but the birth rate stayed high, and each year there were far more births than deaths.

But the birth rate doesn't stay high in an industrial nation. It eventually starts dropping, too, for a number of reasons. In an

A family of sixteen in Paraguay. *Photo: UNICEF; photographer: David Mangurian*

industrialized nation there is a smaller percentage of people living on farms and a larger percentage of people living in cities and working in factories and in offices. There is less useful work children can do in cities. They can work in factories, but that is so harmful to them that all the industrial nations passed laws against such "child labor" after a while.

Not only are children less useful in the city than on a farm, but they are a much greater expense in the city. In an industrial nation, city jobs usually require a certain amount of knowledge. People must be able to read and write, do arithmetic and have other skills as well, whereas on a farm they can do without any of that.

In industrial nations, therefore, there must be schools; and children must go to the schools. This costs money. In the city, too, life is more complex and more expensive in every way.

In short, as a nation grows industrialized, it becomes difficult for parents to support many children. Those with many children find their standard of living is poorer than those with few. More and more people decide to limit the number of children they are to have, for that reason.

Then, too, people in industrial nations begin to see that it isn't necessary to have a great many children, just in case a number of them die in infancy. In an industrial society, fewer and fewer children die, as medicine grows more advanced. Then, too, as nations grow industrialized, social concern for the sick and the aged grows. Such things as pension plans, unemployment insurance, social security, free medical care and so on become more common.

For all these reasons, more and more adults become less and less eager to have many children. The birth rate begins to drop, and nowadays birth rates of less than 25 per thousand per year are common in industrial nations. It has gone as low as 13 per thousand per year in East Germany.

Thus, although the population of Great Britain, for instance, increased so rapidly during much of its period of industrialization, it is now increasing more slowly. This slower increase, brought about by a drop in birth rate, has taken place in other industrialized nations, too.

The manner in which industrial nations pass from very rapid growth rate to a slower growth rate is called the "demographic transition."

If such a thing as the demographic transition takes place, does this mean that we don't have to worry about population after all? Won't the whole world go through the demographic transition after a time? As China, India, Africa and Latin America become industrialized, won't they, too, experience a drop in birth rate and won't world population level off then? And won't that mean everything will be all right?

Unfortunately, it is too late to rely on the demographic transition. The world can't wait for it. In the first place, we can't compare the situation of Europe in 1800 with Asia, Africa and Latin America today. The conditions are entirely different. To see why this is so, let's compare Great Britain in 1800 with India today.

In 1800, Great Britain had a population of 10,000,000 in 240,000 square kilometers, so that its average population density was $24/km^2$. Compare this with India, which, as I said earlier in the book, now has an average population density of $170/km^2$.

India now has seven times as dense a population as Great Britain had at the beginning of its industrialization. India, therefore, begins from a much higher population base and has less room in which to grow.

Another consideration is this. Great Britain in 1800 was part of a world in which the total population was only a quarter of what it is today. Large areas of the world in 1800, particularly in the Americas and in Australia, were still comparatively empty. The British population could emigrate to these comparatively empty lands.

In fact, the population in Great Britain itself has multiplied only a little over five times in the last 200 years. Three-fourths of all the people of British descent do *not* live in Great Britain. They live in the United States, in Canada, in Australia, in New Zealand and so on. There are more than twice as many people of British descent in the United States alone as there are in Great Britain. This is true, to a lesser extent, of the rest of Europe, too. Even as late as the period between 1900 and 1920, no less than 14,000,000 Europeans moved to the United States and to other nations of the American continents.

India and the rest of the nonindustrial world cannot expect to relieve their population pressures by emigration to other regions of the world. There are no longer regions that will accept large numbers of immigrants. If, then, the population of the nonindustrial world multiplies as the population of Great Britain did during its period of industrialization, all the population rise will have to be taken care of at home.

The, too, the death rate in Great Britain and in other European nations fell, as a result of advances in technology and in medicine within those countries. These advances came slowly and the death rate fell slowly. This meant that although the population of Europe, and of Great Britain in particular, rose, it didn't rise as fast as it might have. By the time the death rate had dropped a great deal, the nations were far advanced in industrialization and the birth rate was dropping, too.

The situation is quite different in the nonindustrial world today. In India and in other nonindustrial nations, the advances of the industrial nations are being adopted rapidly. Disinfectants, insecticides, antitoxins, antibiotics, methods for purifying water and disposing of sewage are all adopted.

As a result of this use of products of industrial nations, the death rate was cut to half of what it was, or even less than half, in just a few decades. Meanwhile, since the nation is still nonindustrial and hasn't had a chance to get used to the industrial way of looking at children, the birth rate stays very high.

For this reason, the population growth in India and other nonindustrial nations today is much more rapid than it was for Great Britain and the rest of Europe in 1800.

You see, then, that long before the demographic transition can take place in the nonindustrialized world today, population disaster would have overtaken us. In fact, even if the demographic transition were to take place today, it wouldn't help the situation, really.

As the birth rate fell in the industrial nations, it always stayed ahead of the death rate. The death rate in industrial nations is now at 11 per thousand per year or less. This means that despite the low birth rate in industrial nations, their population growth rate is still about 1 percent per year.

This is below the world average, but it is still considerably higher than it ever was before 1900. Even a 1 percent per year population increase is enough to bring disaster, although not quite as quickly as a 2 percent per year population increase will.

We can't just sit back and do nothing then. We have to do something, and we must do it now. What's more, whatever we do had better be right, because there will be no time left in which to try again.

But *what* do we do?

14

EDUCATION

The first thing that must be done in the face of this terrible population problem, is to educate people. It seems hard to believe that millions of people don't really understand that there is a population problem at all, but it's so.

There are still many people who do not really know anything about the world. They know their own farm, their own village, their own neighbors, nothing more. They must work so hard just to stay alive that they have no time or energy to learn about the world. Even if they wanted to, they have not been educated; they have never been to school; they don't know how to read and write. They are "illiterate."

The percentage of people who can't read or write is declining. Even so, the world population is going up so quickly that even with smaller percentages, each year the number of illiterates increases by 10,000,000. And there are many millions of people who can read and write but do so only with difficulty. Therefore, they don't read much.

Having babies is natural, and people without knowledge of population problems have no notion that such a natural thing can possibly be dangerous. Many of them still think of babies in the old-fashioned way. They think of them as extra hands on the farm and as

support for parents in old age. They think babies show how manly the father is, and so on.

How can the dangers of population growth be explained to them? After all, though they are illiterate, they are human beings who are as important and as intelligent as anyone else. It is not their fault they have had no chance to learn to read and write. Still, because they cannot read and write they can't read a book like this one. Even if someone read it to them, it would still be hard for them to understand. Everything in this book is so far away from their own experience.

Advanced technology may be a help, though. Books and reading aren't as important as they once were. Nowadays, television is a very good tool for education. People can see and hear, as they watch people tell them the dangers of overpopulation in their own language, using examples they can understand, and pictures from their own life.

It would be difficult to set up television stations all over the world, but special satellites spinning around Earth high in space can help. Television waves can be bounced off such satellites so that they can reach any spot in the world. If television sets were made available everywhere, people would watch and learn.

Education will be an important tool to these Iranian girls. *Photo: UNICEF; photographer: Bernard Gerin*

It isn't only those who are completely ignorant who must be taught about the population crisis. There are many people who are educated and who know about the world population and the way it is growing, but think there is no danger. They tell themselves that people who talk of the danger are foolish and wrong.

People who don't believe there is a crisis can point to the Netherlands, for instance. They say that the Netherlands is prosperous and yet is much more densely populated than the world average. They say that it would do no harm to let the whole world become that densely populated. They don't seem to realize that the Netherlands is prosperous because it has fertile soil and much water;

that it makes use of a great deal of industrial products like fertilizer and insecticides; that it imports a great deal of oil and that it has no forests to speak of.

There just isn't enough fertile soil and enough water to make the entire world into one gigantic Netherlands. There isn't enough fertilizer and insecticides and oil, and we don't really want to cut down all the forests. Besides, it won't take very long for the Earth to be as densely populated all over as the Netherlands is now, and if it could be done, how would we stop the population increase at that point?

Some people think that science will solve all problems. They say that more people will just mean more scientists working on those problems. They don't realize that the problems get worse and worse, faster and faster, and that sooner or later—probably sooner—science just won't be able to keep up the pace.

Some people even think that population means strength. They think that large nations with many people can conquer neighboring nations with fewer people. They think that many people means a large, powerful army. They think that if their own nation does not increase its population, a neighboring nation which *does* increase its population will conquer them. For this reason, some nations think that they must have more and more babies, and more and more people if they are to remain strong and free.

Even if war is not involved, some people think a nation with a large population can keep its own customs, language and attitudes better than a nation with a small population. If a neighboring nation grows faster, they think, that neighboring nation might impose *its* customs, language and attitudes on the smaller one, just by outnumbering them.

Actually, this is not so. Very often in history, small nations have conquered large ones. It's not so much the size of the army as its organization, and the technical level of its weapons. Thus, Greece took over Persia in the 300s B.C., Mongolia took over China in the 1200s and Great Britain took over India in the 1700s, even though

Nigerian children are part of an experiment in education television. *Photo: UN / UNESCO / RACCAH Studio*

Persia, China and India were far more populous than Greece, Mongolia and Great Britain.

Then, too, the Greek language and culture in ancient times and the English language and culture in modern times spread over the world even though those languages were spoken by few people to begin with.

If a nation wishes to avoid being dominated by its neighbors, its best chance is to raise its standard of living and its level of technology. This can be done best by not allowing its population to grow to such a point that it is sunk in misery and poverty. In fact, the worst way in which a nation can try to avoid being dominated by its neighbor is to increase its population to the point of misery and poverty.

If every nation tries to compete with its neighbors by raising its population, then the whole world will be sunk in misery and poverty. The nations will all decline in a catastrophe that will leave nothing behind that is worth dominating. No one will have gained anything. Everyone will have lost everything.

Once all this is understood, and people are generally agreed that population growth must not be allowed to continue, they must also come to understand how that growth can be stopped. Population grows because more people are being born than are dying. There are two ways, then, in which the growth can be stopped. You can increase the number of people who die until it matches the number of people who are being born. Or else you can decrease the number of people who are born until it matches the number of people who are dying.

The first method—increasing the death rate—is the usual way in which population is controlled in all species of living things other than ourselves. It is the method by which human populations have been controlled in the past. It is the "natural" method. If there are too many people, some starve or die of disease or by violence. If we don't do anything now, it will be the way population will be controlled in the future. Billions will die.

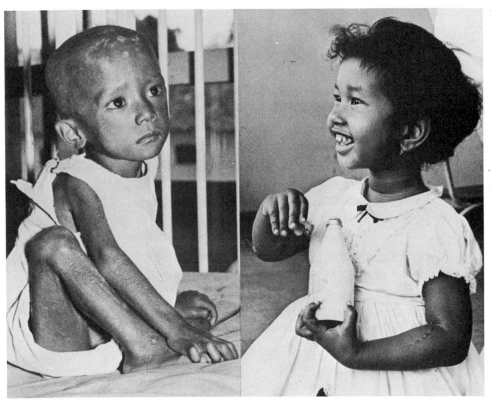

Adequate nutrition makes an enormous difference. *Photos: UNICEF; photographer, left: Jack Ling; photographer, right: Ilsa Kraus*

Must we let that happen because it is the "natural" way?

Through all the history of mankind, the human brain has been bending nature to its will. If we had really decided that the "natural" way was the right way, we would never have begun to make tools, or build fires, or develop agriculture or study science. It is because mankind has bent nature to its will, that there are now many, many people who live more comfortably and better than people ever have before. We must continue to work out ways to be more comfortable by using the intelligent way, and not just the "natural" way.

The "natural" way to control population is by raising the death rate, but we don't want that, for that way lies catastrophe. The intelligent way is to reduce the birth rate. If, say, 40,000,000 people die each year, then not more than 40,000,000 people should be born each year. In fact, we may want to *reduce* the world population to some reasonable value, in which case, if 40,000,000 people die each year, we may want only 30,000,000 people to be born, or only 20,000,000, till the desired population level is reached.

But how can the birth rate be reduced?

One way is for people to stop mating. This, however, is not very practical, since people enjoy it too much to stop. A better way is to let mating continue but to use methods that keep it from resulting in babies.

There are a number of different ways in which the birth rate can be made to drop without interfering with people's pleasure. In the last twenty years, the birth rate in the United States and in some other countries has dropped because more and more women are using pills to keep from having babies they don't want.

To make sure that mating doesn't result in babies is called "birth control." It is by adopting methods of birth control that population growth can be stopped with least damage done.

There are many difficulties here. Certain religious organizations are against birth control. Many groups of people have ways of life that would not fit in easily with birth control. Then, too, even if birth control were desired, there are many places in the world where people are so poor they can't afford to buy the materials that make it possible.

So you see, it comes down to education again. People not only have to be taught that a problem exists, they have to be taught exactly how to solve it by birth control, and why it is right to do so. And they must be given the necessary materials without charge.

Birth control won't stop population growth immediately, of course. It will take time to educate and persuade people to limit births. Fortunately, modern technology offers us new ways to educate and spread information. We now have radio and television. We have communications satellites which can make it possible to reach every part of the world by radio and television. By picture and by spoken word we can even reach the illiterate.

Even with all the means of modern science, though, it will still take time. The growth rate may begin to drop, but it won't get down to zero till 2050 at the earliest, perhaps.

By 2050, the total world population may be about 8,000,000,000. About 1,500,000,000 will be living in the nations now industrialized and 6,500,000,000 in the nations now nonindustrialized. This is perhaps the best we can expect.

If we are to reach the high population of 2050 without disaster and be prepared to reduce the population afterward, there will have to be a number of changes in the world's way of life.

15

CHANGES

If the best we can hope for is that the world population rises to 7,000,000,000 by 2000 A.D. and then stays at that level, more or less, for a century, what will that mean?

It means that the world will have to conserve its energy supplies carefully to make them last until a time of reasonable population and ample energy comes again. This certainly can't be done if people waste energy for harmful reasons, or even for just useless ones. The most common occasion for wasting energy uselessly, or even harmfully, is the hatred and suspicion of one nation for another.

For thousands of years, the world has been divided into separate nations, each of which has thought its own selfish interests to be all that counted. They have rarely hesitated to go to war, each eager to seize what it could of its neighbor's land and goods. One nation has rarely worried about the damage it (or anyone else) might inflict on another nation. The attitude seems always to be: "We are all right, so why need we worry about what happens to another nation?"

Even today, some people think that if their own nation is not too badly crowded, the population crisis is not something they have to worry about, because it is only a crisis for other nations.

But this is no longer a reasonable way to look at the world. Nations can no longer imagine themselves to be separate in this crowded world, so there must be changes in the way people think.

People must learn to realize that if the population growth in one nation upsets the ecology there, the effect spreads out beyond its borders. If one nation produces pollution, that spreads out to the rest of the world. If it uses up resources wastefully, the rest of the world is deprived, too. If it experiences social turmoil, life becomes harder elsewhere.

No industrial nation can expect to keep up its standard of living unless it can trade with the rest of the world. Not one produces all it needs within its own borders. No nonindustrial nation can expect to become industrialized and raise its standard of living without trade with the rest of the world. It's a case of rising together or falling together.

This isn't surprising, considering how small the world is now. Jet planes can take people from any point on Earth to any other point in a few hours. Television can carry a message from any point on Earth to any other point in a few seconds. Compare this to how quickly men could travel and communicate in ancient times, and you will

Part of the United Nations Plaza area. *Photo: United Nations*

see that the whole world is far smaller today than the Roman Empire was in 100 A.D. or Egypt was in 3000 B.C.

It makes no sense for every one of the dozens of nations on Earth to think it can treat itself as a separate world. It is too close to its neighbors for that and it depends too much on its neighbors. It certainly makes no sense for each nation to think that it can use force to protect its interests.

Many of the world's nations spend a great deal of energy in manufacturing weapons of war, or producing goods with which to buy weapons of war. These weapons are useless as long as there is no war, and harmful when there is one. Many of the world's nations keep a great many men in uniform to be ready for war. They, too, are kept in idleness if there is no war and commit great harm if there is one.

It was once possible to fight wars, and some nations raised their own standard of living by conquering and enslaving others. The Romans did so 2,000 years ago, and the European nations grew richer at the expense of their colonies in modern times. The situation, however, has changed. Because of technological advance, wars have become so destructive that they cannot be fought to the profit of anyone. Yet people still act as though wars are possible and waste energy getting ready for war. If mankind is to survive, they must change their old attitudes and make them fit the changed times.

Any war between the Soviet Union and the United States, for instance, would probably involve the use of nuclear weapons on both sides and therefore cannot be fought profitably on either side. Both nations would be destroyed and very likely much of the rest of the world as well.

If either of these two giant nations fights a smaller nation, the other is likely to support the smaller nation. If two smaller nations fight, the Soviet Union is likely to support one, the United States the other. In all these cases, there is always the risk of starting a nuclear war. For that reason if either the Soviet Union or the United States is

Children of many nations proclaim "Peace on Earth" in the General Assembly Hall of the United Nations. *Photo: UPI*

involved in a war, either one is careful not to exert its full strength. If neither is involved, both try to stop a war that breaks out between small nations as soon as they can.

Even if a war between the Soviet Union and the United States were fought without nuclear weapons, it would be unprofitable to either side. The weapons used are so advanced, even when they are not nuclear, and require so much energy to make, to keep in repair and to use, that neither nation could afford the energy to fight a major war.

Consider, then, that wars are suicide, and that the population crisis will destroy civilization if it is not solved. It makes no sense, then, for the powerful nations of the world to concentrate so much of their energy on armies and weapons they can't use, and so little of their energy on efforts to solve the population crisis. The nations are all in one spaceship together—the Earth—and only if they begin to cooperate will they survive their common journey.

There are many people who felt the need for nations to get together during the dark days of World War II. At that time a number of them joined an organization called the "United Nations." More and more nations have joined and now well over a hundred of them belong to the organization.

The United Nations doesn't have much power but it is a meeting place where nations can talk instead of fight. As the crisis gets worse, the United Nations may gain power, as nations see that in united, sensible action is the only hope of survival. In short, then, the nations of the world must disband their armies, abandon their war weapons and, through the United Nations, turn their minds and efforts to the real danger.

If the world's energy supply is to last through the coming crisis, it must not only be conserved, it must be spread out as evenly as possible. If some regions have a great deal of energy, they will be encouraged to use it wastefully. If some regions have great shortage of energy, they cannot develop a decent standard of living.

This means that the industrial nations of the world must voluntarily use less energy in order that more energy be made available to the nonindustrial nations. It means that the standard of living of the rich nations must go down so that the standard of living of the poor nations may go up.

This seems like asking a lot. Why should the well-to-do voluntarily give up what they have?

For one thing, the industrial nations of the world have been powerful enough to trade, on their own terms and to their own profit, with the nonindustrial nations over the last two centuries. The industrial nations have prospered at the expense of the nonindustrial nations in all that time. Isn't it only fair to restore the balance a little now?

Some people might argue that the industrial nations profited because their people were more ingenious, inventive, intelligent, industrious than the people of the nonindustrial nations. They might argue that the industrial nations deserved to prosper and grow rich and should not give it up now.

Even if that were so, it is now impossible for one part of the world to prosper at the expense of another. The world is too small, and the danger for all is too great. Actually, it is to the selfish interest of the industrial nations to be unselfish and give up some of their wealth.

If the industrial nations cling to their standard of living, it may be that the population problem will not be beaten, and that world civilization will collapse. In that case, the present-day industrial nations will, in the end, be far worse off than they would be if they had

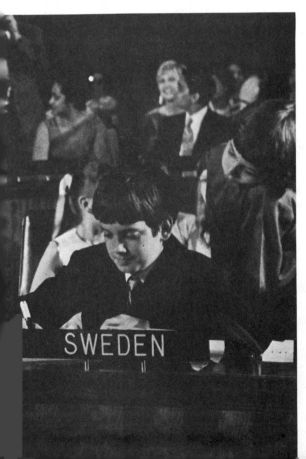

Some of these children may someday solve many of the world's problems. *Photo: UPI*

given up some of their wealth voluntarily when they might have.

By giving up some of their wealth, by sharing out some of their energy, the industrial world will help the nonindustrial nations bring their populations under control. Education alone may not be enough. Knowledge of birth control methods, added to that, may still not be enough.

To make it enough, suppose every effort is made to help the nonindustrial nations raise their standard of living. That means a change in their way of life away from the old customs that tie them to a large family. A new way of life, with greater security, is a much better argument for having fewer children than just words and explanations can be. With better health and better education, the people of the nonindustrial world can contribute more to the welfare of the world, too, and be happier themselves.

And if sharing the wealth helps bring about a halt in the population growth, the whole world, including the industrial nations, will have more chance of surviving the present crisis, and they, too, will be far better off in the long run.

Then if the crisis is beaten, by 2100 A. D. we may have a world population that is declining toward some permanent, safe level. We may also have a world without war, and one that is used to working together. We may have a world that is uniformly prosperous and not one that is divided into rich nations and poor nations.

By 2100 A. D., we should also have new sources of energy that will be fully developed and will be far more permanent and useful than those we have had in the past. There will then be a chance for a new advance to a new level of prosperity during which humanity can truly reach out beyond the Earth to other worlds, and become more powerful and happy than we can imagine today.

—— But only if people conquer the crisis now. Only if they learn to stop population growth by limiting the birth rate. Only if the nations learn to cooperate and to share. Only if we all learn to behave as reasonable and decent human beings.

It is for the children today, and those to come, that we must conserve and protect our resources. *Photo: UPI*

APPENDIX

CONVERSION TABLE

LINEAR MEASURE
1 inch = 2.54 centimeters
0.393700 inches = 1 centimeter
1 mile = 1.60935 kilometers
0.62137 miles = 1 kilometer

SQUARE MEASURE
1 square inch = 6.4516 square centimeters
0.15500 square inches = 1 square centimeter
1 hectare = 2.471 acres
1 square mile = 2.58999 square kilometers
0.3861 square miles = 1 square kilometer

CUBIC MEASURE
1 cubic inch = 16.3871 cubic centimeters
0.061024 cubic inches = 1 cubic centimeter
1 cubic yard = 0.76455 cubic meters
1.30794 cubic yards = 1 cubic meter

LIQUID MEASURE
1 ounce = 2.95729 centiliters
0.33815 ounces = 1 centiliter
1 (U.S.) liquid quart = 0.9463 liters
1.0567 (U.S.) quarts = 1 liter
1 (U.S.) gallon = .0037853 kiloliters
264.179 (U.S.) gallons = 1 kiloliter

WEIGHTS
1 ounce (avoirdupois) = 28.3495 grams
0.035274 ounces (avoirdupois) = 1 gram
1 pound (avoirdupois) = 0.453592 kilograms
2.20462 pounds (avoirdupois) = 1 kilogram
1 (short) ton = 0.90718 (metric) tons
1.10231 (short) tons = 1 (metric) ton
1 pound (avoirdupois) = 1.21528 pounds (troy)
0.82286 pounds (avoirdupois) = 1 pound (troy)

FURTHER READING

Ehrlich, Paul, *The Population Bomb,* 1971, New York, Ballantine Books

Frankel, Lillian B., and Population Reference Bureau, *This Crowded World,* 1970, Washington, D.C., Columbia Books

Fremlin, John, *Be Fruitful and Multiply,* 1977, London, Hart-Davis

Harrison, Harry, *Make Room! Make Room!,* 1973, New York, Berkley Publishing

Hellman, Hal, *Population,* 1972, Philadelphia, J.B. Lippincott

Hyde, Margaret O., *This Crowded Planet,* 1961, New York, McGraw-Hill

Jones, Claire, et al., *Pollution: The Population Explosion,* 1972, Minneapolis, Minn., Lerner Publications

Lowenherz, Robert J., *Population,* 1970, Mankato, Minn., Creative Educational Society

Population Reference Bureau, *World Population Dilemma,* 1967, Washington, D.C., Columbia Books

Pringle, Laurence, *One Earth, Many People: The Challenge of Human Population Growth,* 1971, Riverside, New Jersey, Macmillan Company

Rossman, Isadore, *Two Children by Choice,* New York, Parents Magazine Press

INDEX